KILLER POKER
HOLD'EM HANDBOOK

BOOKS BY JOHN VORHAUS

The Comic Toolbox: How to Be Funny Even If You're Not

Creativity Rules! A Writer's Workbook

The Pro Poker Playbook: 223 Ways to Win More Money Playing Poker

Killer Poker: Strategy and Tactics for Winning Poker Play

Killer Poker Online: Crushing the Internet Game

KILLER POKER
HOLD'EM HANDBOOK

A Workbook for Winners

John Vorhaus

LYLE STUART
Kensington Publishing Corp.
www.kensingtonbooks.com

LYLE STUART BOOKS are published by

Kensington Publishing Corp.
850 Third Avenue
New York, NY 10022

All Kensington titles, imprints, and distributed lines are available at special quantity discounts for bulk purchases for sales promotions, premiums, fund-raising, educational, or institutional use. Special book excerpts or customized printings can also be created to fit specific needs. For details, write or phone the office of the Kensington special sales manager: Kensington Publishing Corp., 850 Third Avenue, New York, NY 10022, attn: Special Sales Department, phone 1-800-221-2647.

Lyle Stuart is a trademark of Kensington Publishing Corp.

First printing: August 2004

10 9 8 7 6 5 4 3 2

Printed in the United States of America

ISBN 0-8184-0641-0

Dedicated to the millions of cockeyed optimists
who still believe that any two will do.

Contents

Foreword

by Annie Duke

Being part of the poker world these days makes me think of what it must have been like in the NBA at the beginning of its rise to phenomenal popularity. Even if you can't dunk a basketball, it's a pretty heady feeling the first time you realize that the sky is, indeed, the limit. With the World Poker Tour garnering staggering ratings on the Travel Channel and ESPN's coverage of the World Series of Poker breaking records for its time slot, poker as a spectator—and participant!—sport has truly arrived. For anyone with some history in this game, it's an almost inconceivable turn of events. When I first started playing in the WSOP, for example, I could never have even imagined a field of 839 entrants ponying up $10K each to play. Yet that's exactly what we had in 2003. Like the man said, "Who'da thunk it?"

It wasn't always like this, of course, and I can tell you when it was almost exactly *not* like this: the mid-1990s, when I and a straggly group of other poker players and writers got together and said, "Hey, you know, there might be something to this poker business after all." In a classic case of putting our money where our mouths were, we launched a highly regarded and wildly ill-fated magazine called *Poker*

World. I had the honor of editing that magazine, and I'm here to tell you it was a thing of beauty: a glossy, high-class monthly cut from the same cloth as *Cigar Aficionado* or even *GQ*.

It was a thrilling time in my life. I had just had my first baby, and now here I was, involved in this incredibly exciting project that allowed me to express and invoke the creative artiste living deep beneath my rough-and-tumble poker exterior. At the same time, it was a constant struggle managing a magazine with too tight a budget in a time when no one outside our small circle of friends could see (or cared to pay for) the potential that poker offered.

Poker World was ahead of its time, arriving before the introduction of televised poker and, especially, internet poker, the advertising cash cow that would certainly have kept our little enterprise afloat. Although we poker players who lived for the game firmly understood the appeal of poker, the advertising and distribution companies did not, and the magazine went the way of most fledgling periodicals: under.

It was during these darkish days that I first met John Vorhaus. Not only is John a wonderful and funny man, a great writer, and an even greater friend, he also shared the vision that poker done right could capture the public's imagination. He was a monthly contributor to *Poker World* and I can honestly say that his stories were the most enjoyable for me to read—and the easiest to edit, I might add. As the storm clouds gathered around the foundering good ship *Poker World,* John offered a constant and unrelenting ray of sunshine.

Despite the pressures of running *Poker World* and the understandable relief I felt when it was finally taken off life support, I missed that damn magazine for a long, long time, much the way an amputee misses a missing limb. I especially missed John's witty and articulate contributions, and, selfishly, missed having an excuse to talk to him on a regular basis when deadlines loomed. That's why I was so excited and honored when he asked me to write this Foreword—in no small part because it has given us an excuse to yack together again, just like old times.

But I must tell you that talking poker with John Vorhaus is a little like, to quote Billy Bragg, "talking to the tax man about poetry." He just comes at it from such a different point of view. Where most of your poker writers (and poker players) have an almost fetishistic obsession with pot odds and win rates and expected value, John seems to . . . I don't know what the word is . . . wait, no, yes I do: It's "inhabit." John seems to *inhabit* the game. He sees poker from the inside out. More to the point, he sees poker's deep connections to the life a person lives. He offers us perspective.

If you're coming to this book for specific advice about specific hold'em situations, you won't be disappointed, because there's plenty here to satisfy the most fanatic play-of-hand junkie. But if all you get out of the book is advice about situations, I put it to you that you're not digging quite deeply enough, either into the book or into your own poker play. After all, poker doesn't take place in a vacuum (as any mother of four on the tournament trail will haggardly attest!) and John asks—I think he demands—that you put your play in the context of your own life and livelihood. I wouldn't go so far as to call this book a spiritual journey, but okay, yeah, maybe I would.

Talking of spiritual journeys, I remember a column that John wrote years and years ago—years before he ever wrote for me. Its title was *If You Meet Buddha on the Road, Kill Him,* and it cautioned us not to get too carried away with what mentors or experts had to say. At a time when I was just starting to devise my own, if you will, poker philosophy, I was struck by the profoundly sensible nature of this suggestion. Expert play, John postulated, came not from mindless memorization of start charts or odds tables, but from learning how to really think about the game you play. "Be your own teacher," John suggested, wise counsel that has stuck with me from that day to this.

While this book doesn't specifically revisit the concept of killing the Buddha, I think you could do worse, while you're reading it, than to keep that thought in mind. In a game like poker, after all, where the best advice is always "it depends," you can no more expect to follow any rote set of instructions to poker glory than to follow any self-appointed Buddha to nirvana. At the end of the day, the only real Buddha is the Buddha within.

Cripes, now *I'm* sounding all spiritual. So I think I'll just shut up and let you read the book. Don't just read it, though. Try to experience it . . . inhabit it. If you let yourself go, I think you'll be a different player coming out than you were going in. And not just a different one. A better one, too.

ANNIE DUKE is the leading woman money winner in World Series of Poker events.

Acknowledgments

Much of this book was written covertly. Notebook in hand, I sat in hold'em games for hours on end, feverishly recording everything I saw, heard, felt, or thought for later processing into prose. In that sense, my myriad opponents have been unwitting contributors to the cause. Of course I can't thank all of them personally, since I know so few of them by name. A few more I know by private nickname: secret handles like Tillman, Doctor Depresso, and Tiger Shark that I award to certain players to remind me how they play. Most have remained anonymous foes, and that's as it should be, for while a poker table is a social setting to be sure, it's much more a place to make money than friends. Nor, on the other hand, is it necessary to thank them all, since in many cases I paid them for the information I got. Playing perfect poker while also taking comprehensive notes, I discovered, can be dismayingly hard.

I want to thank my wife, Maxx Duffy, for her ongoing support. She's been with me through my whole Rake's Progress of poker, not just this book but all the books and not just these poker sessions but all the sessions. If she saw these latest pages as a bald-faced excuse for me to *play more poker,* well, she cut me some slack, for which slack I was, am, and always will be grateful.

Many readers of *Killer Poker* and *Killer Poker Online* have taken the time to email me and tell me how much they enjoyed and appreciated those books. Thank you for thanking me. You inspire me to write on.

Introduction

Before we get started, let's spend a moment on definition of terms, just so we're all, you know, reading from the same page.

The topic of discussion in this book is *fixed limit Texas hold'em*, as commonly played in the public cardrooms and casinos of America. "Fixed limit" refers to the mandated betting structure of the game: Players may only bet a single unit on the first and second betting rounds, and may only bet a double unit on the third and fourth betting rounds. In a game of $10–$20 fixed limit (or just limit) Texas hold'em (or just hold'em), then, you'd make bets and raises in $10 increments before and after the flop, and in $20 increments on the so-called turn and river.

Another common feature of limit hold'em is the forced bet, or *blind*. With each deal of the cards, the first and second players are required to post a blind bet in order to create a pot worth fighting for. Typically these forced bets, the *small blind* and *big blind*, are one half and one whole single betting unit; thus $5 and $10 respectively in a $10–$20 fixed limit game. After each deal, the position of the blinds advances one player, so that each combatant in turn faces his fair share of these must-play situations.

I know you know all this, but bear with me.

If you've watched poker tournaments on TV anytime recently (and there's been an explosion of same in the last couple of years), you've no doubt seen a different version of Texas hold'em—*no-limit hold'em*—where players may bet any or all of their chips at any time. No-limit hold'em is an endlessly fascinating game, the strategy and tactics for which fall generally outside the scope of this book. For deep insight into no-limit hold'em or no-limit tournament hold'em, I suggest you read *Championship No-Limit & Pot Limit Hold 'Em* by T. J. Cloutier and Tom McEvoy or *Tournament Poker for Advanced Players* by David Sklansky. Both books will arm you well for combat in that arena.

Limit hold'em, meanwhile, is the single most popular form of poker played today, far surpassing former contenders such as seven-card stud, draw, and lowball. With its simplicity of play and opportunities for psychological warfare, it appeals to players with all different types of strengths: Math wonks love it; so do bluffers. People readers find it profitable, and the sit-back-and-wait-for-cards crowd can prosper, too. It's much more generally popular than its no-limit counterpart for the simple reason that it's not quite so easy for bad players to go broke. In no-limit games, unskilled players stand very little chance against the experts. They don't last long, so the game doesn't last long. Limit structure levels the playing field, and it is on this very popular level playing field that Texas hold'em has found a home.

It is a home, needless to say, unlike the home poker games that many people grew up on. Most home games are wide open affairs where dealers call the game, wild cards come and go, and camaraderie counts more than conquest. These are fun gatherings, but, again, outside the scope of this book. What limit hold'em does is *limit* the players' options, and provides them a forum for testing themselves against one another in a neatly balanced, nicely constrained way. As Elvis Presley once told me in a dream, "The rules don't confine, they define." This is particularly true of limit hold'em where, in the context of a closely defined set of rules, there's an infinite palate of strategic and tactical choice.

So, okay, we're talking limit hold'em here. We're not talking bet-the-farm no-limit tournaments, and we're not talking one-up-two-up-high-low-strawberry like you used to play with Granny.

Okay, now that we've got that out of the way, let's go back in time.

I gave my first public poker lecture at the Maxim Casino in Las Vegas in 1990. If memory serves, there were no more than a dozen people in a dismayingly large and echoey hotel ballroom, and memory may, in fact, be exaggerating that number. Given what I knew about poker at the time, that was probably a dozen too many listeners, anyhow. To put it one way, the reach of my enthusiasm had exceeded the grasp of my expertise. To put it another way, I was just totally out of my depth. No problem. "If you can't be right, be loud," say some. "If you're loud enough long enough, you will eventually appear to be right." That sure was the strategy I was pushing that night.

In poker we call this bluffing.

Maybe you think I was out of line, or possibly out to lunch, for giving that speech in the first place, but I don't think so. As a teacher I've always been an avid learner, and part of my approach has been to say, "Hey, I don't quite understand this either, so let's all work together to figure it out." In this case, though I was representing a hand I didn't have, I managed to sell the bluff successfully. I had that audience of one dozen (or fewer) eating right out of my hand—right up until the moment I threw the floor open to questions. That's when someone stood up and asked how I thought he should play J-T offsuit in early position. I remember the deer-in-headlights terror I felt as I realized, "I have no idea what this guy's talking about." I understood the words, but I had played so little hold'em up to that point, and had so little grasp of the game, that I just had no intelligent answer at hand.

But, like a player with bottom pair and a back-door flush draw, I was not entirely without outs. In particular, I had the Socratic Method to fall back on. The Socratic Method promotes a "teach by asking" strategy, and that's the strategy I turned to then.

"Interesting question," I said. "What would *you* do? How do *you* think J-T offsuit should be played?"

And no, I wasn't evading the question.

Well, okay, yes I was. But also, I was inviting the questioner to think about—really think about—that hold'em situation, and supply some analysis of his own. This not only gave him some insight he previously hadn't had (insight derived, of course, no thanks to me) but also gave him some practice in analyzing his own play.

Having played a couple million hands of hold'em since then, and having written a couple million words about poker, I feel that I'm on much more solid ground now than I was back then. I still can't tell you how to play J-T offsuit in early position, of course, because I don't know your style of play or the opponents you face. I don't know your table image, how you've been running, how you play after the flop, whether you're likely to face raises, and half a dozen other things I absolutely need to know before I can absolutely tell you what to do with the hand.

What I *can* tell you—and teach you—is how to think about this and other hold'em situations, so that when you find yourself in the game, you can come armed with a deeper understanding, and better analytical tools, than the foes you face. That's a margin we can make money on.

And that's what this book will lean on, at least in part. I'm going to ask you to think about your hold'em game and show you, if I can, how to think about it more effectively. Really, all you have to do is think about it *at all* and you'll be a better player than most.

First, though, let's explore what kind of player you are right now. I don't know for sure, but I can make an educated guess or two.

In all likelihood, you're not a professional poker player. You're a keen hobbyist or avid amateur. You play poker for fun and hopefully for profit, but you don't make your living at it. You're a low- to mid-limit player now, but you've been moving up and you plan to continue moving up. You consider it important to play poker as well as you can; you hope and plan to reap the benefits of your dedication. You're more concerned with performance than with outcome, because you know that while bad decisions may occasionally back into good outcomes, only solid, correctly played poker will lead to positive long-term results.

You track your results. You know how you've performed over time, not because you're obsessed with red ink and black, but because you know that no poker player can call himself serious-minded unless he keeps an accurate accounting of his losses and his wins. You desire to earn the title of *Winner*, and you want to back that claim with *proof*, not some fuzzy anecdotal "evidence" that implies you quit winners most of the time.

You don't win all the time. You don't expect to. You hate to lose, but you don't fall into the trap of trying to "get even" or "get well" when the cards aren't breaking your way. You recognize that all of your poker sessions eventually fuse into one (life)long session, and you strive to put your final number on the plus side of the tally board. You try to be a better player every day, and you recognize that through study and thoughtful analysis, you can achieve this reasonable goal.

You go on tilt a lot less often than you did when you first started playing, but still there are times when control of your game slips away. Then again (because you read about poker, and think and talk about poker) you're not the sort of player who's pretty much always on tilt. Though you know those who are. You recognize their perpetual state of mental imbalance: impaired through ignorance, compulsion, or rage. You thank God, or your own strength of will, that you're not like them.

Above all, you *enjoy* your poker. You enjoy the look and feel of cards and chips. You enjoy the cardroom environment. You relish the combat of poker. You appreciate the challenge of playing your best, and of besting your foes. You play to win because winning gets you off, and because winning lets you stay in the game.

You get support from your family, and you have learned that the more seriously you take your play, the more likely you are to get that support. It's not a matter of coming home with big piles of loot; it's a matter of coming home in control, of demonstrating that *you play poker* and *poker doesn't play you*. Poker is your hobby and your mad avocation, but it's not your habit, and it's certainly not your addiction. To borrow from the beer ads, you know when to say when.

At the same time, you have a certain restless ambition when it comes to your game. You want more: more skills and abilities; more financial reward; more triumph. You dream of competing in the World Series of Poker, partly for the glory and partly to test yourself against the best. In the meantime, you play in small and moderate buy-in tournaments for the play and challenge they offer, and for the chance of a sizeable payday.

You have more than a casual understanding of Texas hold'em. You've read enough and played enough to have a sound basic sense of the game. You know what starting requirements are; you have yours, though you don't always abide by them. You have a grasp of such concepts as pot odds, and know what it means to be betting with the best of it. You've won with bad cards. You've lost with good cards. You've been around the block.

As much as you know about hold'em, you also know what you don't know. You know that some players just seem to have a natural gift for the game, a knack for knowing how to take control of a tournament table or live-action game. You admire these players, and ever so slightly envy their knack. You feel it's a knack you lack, and so in the absence of knack, you rely on diligence, discipline, study, and skill. You hope and trust that books like this can help you close the gap between the player you are and the player you plan to be.

Why do I believe that these things are true about you? Because I know absolutely that they're true about me. Though I'm a net-plus player in California's cardrooms for as long as I've kept records (into my second decade now) I don't consider myself to be naturally gifted. I don't take control of every table I sit at. I don't always bring my A game. I haven't won the World Series of Poker. These may seem like strange admissions from the author of a poker book, a so-called expert. Should I not fear that such admissions will undercut the authority by which I write and teach?

Not really, no. Because I know where my authority comes from. My right to write, so to speak, comes directly from sympathy and empathy with my reader; from understanding your approach to the game in relation to my own. I teach, in other words, not from ahead or above, but beside and within. My bottom line and yours are the same. We both want to improve. I have found that writing books like this helps me improve, just as you have found that reading them, *participating* in them, helps you.

Let's be clear about one thing: There are no geniuses here. If you were a genius, you wouldn't need *Killer Poker*. You'd already have all the strategies and skills and success you require. If I were a genius, I wouldn't bother writing. I'd have all the strategies and skills and success I require, too. But I've already confessed that teaching helps me learn, and I've already given away my secret. The secret of asking questions.

So let's get started. Because we've got a lot of ground to cover, and there's a juicy hold'em game out there somewhere just waiting for us to come and kill it.

KILLER POKER
HOLD'EM HANDBOOK

1

♣ ♠ ♦ ♥

MINDSET

♧ ♤ ◇ ♡

Triumph in hold'em happens one hand at a time. The correct decision you make on *this* bet against *this* foe in *this* situation is the foundation upon which all your poker successes stand. Many people think otherwise. They have trouble seeing that one loose call here or one slim draw there can really impact their long-term results. To them I would present the following brief inner dialogue.

What a terrible bet I just made.
            I swear I'll never do that again.
I really misplayed that whole hand.
            Next hand I've got to play right.
God, what a miserable session today.
            Let's hope tomorrow goes better.
This whole week was a waste.
            Next week, though, I just know I'll get well.
Last month was a horror show.
            But it's a new month now.
I've been running bad all year.
            Next year I'm bound to run good.
The last five years were a nightmare.

1

But the next five years will be great.
It seems like I've been running red my whole career.
How can I turn that around?
With the very next bet.
I can start to play right on the very next bet.

In the course of this book we'll examine a whole lot of hold'em situations and discuss performance strategies specific to those moments. But here at the outset, I want you to think mindset. I want you to recognize that your overall hold'em performance is utterly dependent on your overall hold'em state of mind. There is no room for careless thinking; there can be no tolerance for whims or hunches or other such fatuous chinks in your hold'em armor. There must be only peak performance, bet after bet, hand after hand, session after session, hour after day after week after month after year for as long as you play the game.

It's not such a tough goal to achieve. I can boil its essence down to three simple words:

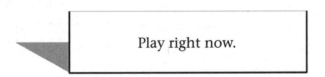

Play right now.

In fact, let's let that be the theme of this book. *Play right now.* If you just make the correct play, to the best of your understanding and abilities, and always endeavor to deepen your understanding and extend your abilities, everything else will take care of itself.

HIDDEN ASSUMPTIONS

What does everyone know about hold'em? What ten things can you think of that everyone who plays hold'em generally holds to be true? I ask the question for two reasons. First, it's a hold'em skill to be able to see the game as others see it, so you can start to transcend their approach and dominate them with an approach of your own. Second, I want you to start thinking *in depth* and *in detail* about the hold'em game you play, and the game you see played around you. I want you to start honing, if you will, your hold'em perception.

So go ahead and generate that list: Ten things we all know about hold'em. I'll do mine in a moment, but I want you to go first, so we can compare notes and see where our opinions converge or diverge. Remember, these are only opinions. There are no absolute right or wrong answers. (For my money, the only wrong answer is not doing the exercise at all.) Don't spend a lot of time or skull-sweat—just answer off the top of your head. Record your answer either here in the space provided, in the notes section at the end of the book or, better still, in a notebook or computer file that you dedicate to the purpose.

Did you do the list? Good. You now have a little more information than you had before, and you also have a little more experience (maybe even your first experience) in thinking about your poker in an orderly, articulate way. You're moving toward clarity of thought.

If you didn't generate the list, may I ask why not? Did you imagine that it was sufficient just to think about the question in a casual way? It's not, you know: If you want to build muscle mass, you have to spend time in the gym; if you want to bulk up your poker muscles, you have to work them out, too. So if you have doubts about the utility of this exercise, or these exercises, I would ask you to suspend your disbelief and just go ahead and do them. I promise they'll pay dividends. Not immediate ones, perhaps, and perhaps not the ones you expected, but they will help your game. I guarantee it.

Okay, here are ten things I think everyone knows about hold'em:

- A-A is the best hold'em hand.
- 2-7offsuit is the worst hold'em hand.
- Position is important.
- Draws play better against many opponents.
- Don't slow-play aces!
- Most players who call one bet call two.
- Suited cards are better than unsuited ones.
- Many players give suited cards too much credit.
- Weak aces are danger hands.
- People think they're better players than they are.

So, do we agree? Disagree? If we disagree, how do we disagree? Are there items on my list that make you say, *Oh, yeah, that's true, too?* Or do you find yourself saying, *Nope, in my experience, that's not so?* Everyone has their own experience of hold'em (and of everything) and this exercise merely serves to demonstrate that "What you see depends on where you stand." No one plays purely objective poker. Everyone invests in their own subjective reality. Everyone. When you can see the game from your opponent's point of view—climb inside his subjective reality, so to speak—you have insight into his play that is stronger and more reliable than any physical tell.

Glancing back at my list of "ten things we all know about hold'em," I note the sentence with the exclamation point: *Don't slow-play aces!* In re-reading that sentence, I have to ask myself a question: Do I really think that most people know this about hold'em, or do I just assume they do because it's an important idea to me? I *do* think it's important; in my subjective reality, slow-playing aces is almost always a big mistake with immediate tragic consequences. This is my *belief*. But if I project that belief onto the hold'em community at large—if I assume that everyone else thinks like me—I'm making a different, much more global mistake. I'm acting according to a *hidden assumption,* the assumption that everyone thinks like me.

Without critical examination, we all act according to our hidden assumptions, *whether those assumptions are valid or not.* If you assume that players defend their blinds too liberally, you will attack more aggressively. You may be right, and you may profit from the move. But if you're wrong, and you leave your assumptions untested, you'll be stepping into errors that you don't even know you're making. And so we come to a new rule for hold'em, a rule that has something to do with the play of given hands, but everything to do with our overall approach to the game:

Test hidden assumptions.

Not only test them, but challenge them, confront them, constantly reappraise them, and then update them in the light of new information.

Go back to your list of things people know about hold'em and ask yourself which, if any, of your entries can be regarded as untested assumptions. Don't feel badly if some are. I remind you that there are no wrong answers here. There's only experimentation, evaluation, and thoughtful examination.

Hidden assumptions lead to lazy thinking. Or no, not exactly that; rather, hidden assumptions create a hospitable environment for laziness to take root and grow. If you *assume* you're going to win, you don't bother with your best game. If you *assume* your foes are too loose, you relinquish your own rigorous discipline. If you *assume* there won't be any traffic en route to the club, you don't bother tuning in a traffic report on the radio. Then you're stuck: stuck in traffic or stuck in a poorly performing mindset or stuck in a game you can't beat.

How do you defeat hidden assumptions? Just be aware of them. Bring them to the surface of your thinking, where you can reflect on them productively. Once you've done that, you can start to gauge their validity (for not all assumptions are invalid) and refine your strategies accordingly.

But first you have to get them out in the open. Let me paint a picture:

I join a game in progress and as I'm settling in I notice half a dozen empty beer bottles on the service table beside me. Now I pick up my first hand, pocket kings, and raise and re-raise until I get heads-up with the player to my right. After a flop of A-K-x, I glance over and detect a certain glazed look in the eye of the player to my right. Unconsciously, I perform the following addition:

$$\begin{array}{r} 6 \text{ empty bottles} \\ + 2 \text{ glazed eyes} \\ \hline 1 \text{ drunk} \end{array}$$

Whipping out my drunk devaluator, I now overestimate his drunken recklessness and underestimate the real strength of his hand. Sad little me when it turns out that he's got pocket aces. That's why he had a glazed look: He was stunned by the awesomely favorable flop. And the beer bottles? They belonged to the player who had my seat before me.

This is an extreme example, but it illustrates the kind of trouble your hidden assumptions can get you into. Fortunately, there's an easy way out. Instead of assuming that the guy is drunk, and acting on that untested assumption, simply tell yourself, "Well, he may be drunk. I'll look for evidence that he is, and then, if I find it, adjust my play accordingly."

Can you think of a circumstance in which your hidden assumptions caused you to misjudge aspects of a certain hold'em game or aspects of the players in it?

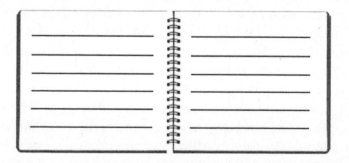

On the other hand, can you think of a time when your assumptions were dead-on accurate?

*Last night I saw a player buy into a $6–$12 hold'em game
with just $60. I assumed that he was more afraid to lose
than eager to win. Sure enough, when I applied pressure, he
folded, in every sense of the word. My assumption—that
short buy-in equaled scared buy-in—was functionally sound.*

When it comes to the play of hands, assumptions impact hold'em in a way that they don't, for example, impact
seven-card stud. In stud, with each player's up-cards available for inspection, you often don't need to make assumptions about their holdings. If they have four to a straight,
that's four to a straight. If they're showing trips, you don't
need to wonder: They have strong cards.

Hold'em, though, *requires* assumptions, and therein lies
the trap. Holding a pair of queens and facing a king on the
flop, you have to make some assumptions—we call them
"guesses"—about whether there are kings out against you.
But can you trust your assumptions? Nope. Not unless you
test them and track them and question them as an ongoing
part of your game.

Suppose we're looking at a flop like T♥-2♥-5♥. When
our foe bets, we might assume he has the flush. We know
from the odds charts in *Killer Poker: Strategy and Tactics for
Winning Poker Play* that the odds are 118-1 against flopping
a flush. The overwhelming majority of the time, then, we're
wrong to assume the made flush. But still the coordinated
look of the flop betrays us. The suited board looks so much
like a flush that, unless we guard against our untested assumptions, we tend to believe that the bettor has that hand.

Then again, there are times when you can—must—trust
the assumptions you make. Consider a flop of T♦-3♦-6♣.
Four people see the flop and everyone checks. Now the
turn card comes, A♦, and the first person to act bets out. If
the turn card had been an ace *or* a diamond, you might rea-

sonably conclude that he's on a steal, but the A♦ fits the board two ways (and is thus twice as apt to have helped one of the players yet to act), making it unlikely that the lead bettor would try to drive a bluff into the full field. From this you can assume—or conclude, if you like—that the lead bettor has at least some piece of this pie.

You can use your opponents' untested assumptions against them. If you know, for example, that they'll be scared by a scary board, you can bet into them—own the scary board, as it were—and let their own hidden assumptions lead them to the conclusion that you have them beaten and they must fold. This isn't even bluffing, really. It's just taking advantage of a certain situation and a certain foe's tendency.

Returning to the example above, where the board comes heart-heart-heart, let's say that you're first to act, and you bet. Maybe your opponent won't fold here. Maybe he knows about the 118-1 odds against flopping a flush. But you did bet, and even if he doesn't put you on a flush, his tendency toward untested assumptions could very well lead him to put you on a flush *draw.* Roughly 20 percent of the time, the next card off the deck will be a heart as well. Be ready to bet that one time out of five, no matter what cards you hold. Let your opponent's aggregate assumptions (you didn't flop a flush *but* you did flop a flush draw *and* your draw got there on the turn) lead him to lay down his hand. It won't always work, nor should you always try it; your opponents may be too bright, or alternatively, too dim to do what you want them to do, or they may themselves have the flush. But the fact remains that if you're thinking about the game in the light of assumptions, both yours and your foe's, you'll be thinking about the game at a higher level than those who read only hands and boards.

Wheels within wheels, right? And wheels within wheels

within wheels within wheels. Without too much effort at all, you can get into the disconcerting mindset of "I think that he thinks that I think that *he* thinks that *I* think . . ." and that way lies madness, or at least clouded thinking. So do this: Neither trust all assumptions nor challenge all assumptions. Simply be aware that assumptions exist in every player's play. Minimize the impact of hidden assumptions on your own play, and maximize the strategic advantage that other players' untested assumptions give you.

You can benefit from practice in this area. Next time you play poker, have your notebook with you and make a list of all the untested assumptions you see flying around.

Deuces never loses. All-in always wins. You always *catch runner-runner! The dealer hates me. It's impossible to beat the rake. All those* [fill in the ethnic blank] *are crazy gamblers.*

Try it for yourself and see.

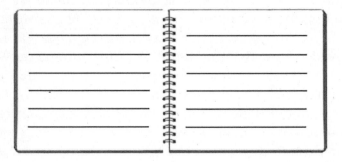

You'll be amazed at how much real insight, and how many holes in other people's games, you can glean from knowing not what your opponents hold, but what they hold to be true.

RIGHT MIND

You're in the third hour of an otherwise unremarkable hold'em session when you pick up pocket tens on the button. It's folded around to you and you raise. The small blind folds and the big blind calls. You have a confident read on your opponent: This guy won't defend his blind with just nothing, even if he puts you on a pure real estate raise. So when the flop comes 9-6-2, you like your hand a lot. You bet for value. Your opponent calls. The turn is a 4, which doesn't scare you because you know the big blind won't have gotten this deep into the hand with swill like 5-3. You bet again, fully expecting your opponent to lay it down now, but he calls. What could he have? A good 9? If he had a set, you'd have heard about it by now.

The river is a queen. The big blind checks and you check too, because a queen is an overcard he could easily have held and hit. Sure enough, he turns over the winning hand of A-Q and takes the pot.

You replay the hand quickly in your head and emerge from your brief analysis satisfied that you played every street correctly, from your preflop raise to your river check. But something about the hand irks you. Your foe called all the way with just overcards. Does he not *respect* you? *What does a guy have to do around here to get these mooks to fold?!* That thing that irks you is now like a raspberry seed stuck in your tooth. The more you think about it, the more it bothers you. It's hard enough to play correctly, you tell yourself, but when you play absolutely correctly and end up suffering for others' mistakes, well, damn, that's just not fair.

A subtle shift has taken place in your thinking. For one thing, you have mentally accused your opponent of having made a mistake when, in fact, his play may have been correct. He held A-Q, after all. You could easily have been on a pure steal (tell me you've never raised on the button with A-T) and even if you weren't, he still had outs. If anything, he might have played the hand too weakly; the river bet went begging, after all. But that's not the problem.

The problem is you've swapped thoughtful analysis for righteous indignation. Your thinking is now colored by your mood. In an otherwise unremarkable hold'em session, you have reached a pivotal point. If you don't get your mind right here, the whole session could go right down the drain. If you continue to dwell on mistakes—which weren't even *your* mistakes—you run the risk of blowing a hole in your concentration, and thence, your stack.

Let's say you pass the test. You shrug off the loss and play the next hand. Lo and behold, you get pocket aces— and they don't hold up. Next hand, pocket kings—and they don't hold up, either! Now you've been hit by a devastating combination of punches. You're suffering at the hands of other players' decisions and also the capricious whims of luck. Your steely discipline is in vapors now. All you can think about is *how damn much you hurt.*

When this happens, you lose. Win or lose, you lose, because as soon as you start to process your pain, you've left your right mind behind and entered the realm of feeling. You're suffering, and when you're suffering you shift your focus from playing perfect poker to wondering why the universe is so unfair. On the conscious level, of course, you know that the universe is not unfair. You know that you're just experiencing a short-term setback. Nevertheless, you *are* experiencing that setback, and you're experiencing it on an emotional level, in an emotional way. You are, in other words, *feeling* the moment rather than *thinking* the moment. Once your situation starts to affect your mood, performance suffers and further bad outcomes may result.

You know this—you *know* this—but let's represent it graphically just the same, just to make it easy to grasp.

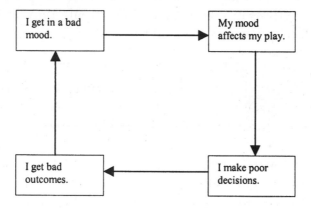

Nor does it necessarily take a bad beat to put you in a bad mood. I remember once in the early, early days of my playing career—I had just graduated from $1–$2 to $2–$4—when I took a break from playing to check the messages on my answering machine at home. The news was not good: A lawsuit I thought had been settled turned out not to be settled and suddenly a 10,000-dollar obligation hung over my head. I went right back into that $2–$4 game and blew off a hundred bucks. That's how upset I was!

You might say I had my priorities screwed up, and you might be right. The ten grand was much more important to me than the $100. But *thinking* about that ten grand, *feeling* the pain of it, cost me a hundred dollars I didn't need to lose.

The memory haunts me still.

Which is, of course, exactly where I go wrong.

There's nothing wrong with holding on to memories of plays that didn't work out. There's certainly nothing wrong with holding on to the memory of mistakes we've made, for that's how we avoid making those mistakes the next time. But if we hold on to *feelings*, if we hold on to *regret*, if we carry these emotions even from one hand to the next, we don't have right mind and we can't expect to win.

For success in hold'em, then (or in any form of poker, or, for that matter, in life), do this:

> Focus on how you do,
> not on how you feel.

That goes for your good feelings, too. If you've been running exceptionally well, if you've been running all over the table, you run the real risk of getting high on your own success. Rushes are real, God bless them, but nothing kills a rush faster than the carelessness that overconfidence breeds. Many a rush has gone south because the player stopped thinking about the useful question—*How can I parlay this rush and my temporarily strong image into a big win?*—and instead turned his attention to *How can I make this good feeling last?*

On the other hand, what's wrong with feeling good? Isn't that part of why we play poker in the first place? We love the game. We want to enjoy the experience of playing it. Yet the more we experience our enjoyment, the less we think about proper play. Performance degrades, and enjoyment ends. We are thus left with a twisted little paradox: To fuel your enjoyment of poker, you must ignore your enjoyment of poker. Later, after your triumphant session, you can bask in the glow of your own good play. But right there, in *that* moment, in *that* hand, how you feel must be the last thing on your mind.

So how do we banish our feelings? I can think of a couple of strategies, but before I get to mine, I would ask you

What are yours? When you feel emotion taking control of your game, what tactics do you use—or could you use—to return yourself to right mind?

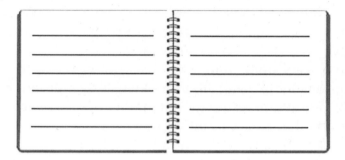

When I find myself going down the road of *feeling* instead of *thinking,* here are a couple of the tricks I use to return myself to right mind.

Think like a closer. A closer in baseball is a pitcher who comes into the game to get the final outs, to close out the win. These hurlers routinely perform in high-stress situations with runners on base and the game on the line. Those who succeed in this role have, or at least claim to have, no different feelings after a win than after a loss. They can't afford to! If they felt the triumph of victory with any kind of intensity, they'd have to feel the agony of defeat with similar intensity, and this intensity of feeling would render them utterly incapable of doing their job. Applying this notion to hold'em, we can tell ourselves to think like a closer, cutting ourselves off from our highs and lows alike. This application of ice water to veins may not seem like such fun, but it improves our performance, and that's what it's all about.

Eyes on the horizon. If you've ever been seasick aboard ship, you've probably heard some well-meaning fellow passenger tell you to stare at the horizon. Looking at something in the far distance, they say, will help to settle your stomach. I don't know about that—it seems my stomach has a mind of its own—but I do know that looking at the horizon can be very helpful in settling my unsteady poker mind. Whether I'm feeling too giddy or too bleak, I can dampen both feelings by consciously putting them in the context of the long arc of my poker career. Ten, twenty, thirty years from now, whatever's going on right now won't matter to me at all. By looking at such distant horizons I am able to reduce the importance of *what's happening now* and thus reduce its influence over me.

Avoid bad neighborhoods (1). There's a rueful expression that goes, "When I'm in my head, I'm in a bad neighborhood." Sometimes my state of mind is actively hazardous to my bankroll. At such times, the best thing I can do is *just not play*. For example, if I'm running bad in a game at a given limit, I might find myself tempted to move up to a higher limit, hoping quickly to undo the damage I've done. There are, of course, times when moving up is a good idea, but this isn't one of them, because right now I'm *feeling* and not *thinking*, and I'm trying to relieve my bad feelings by getting back to even. That's taking a walk down a dark street in a bad neighborhood. I'm just begging to get mugged.

P.R.O. (the positive reinforcement override). I've never been a good golfer, but when I get down on myself, my generally substandard golf game goes in the absolute crapper. I become overwhelmed by the feeling that *I can't do this,* which feeling, sadly, reinforces itself with continued bad play. To escape from this vicious cycle, I simply think about something I'm good at. My self-confidence gets a boost (*You may suck at* this, *but you don't suck at* everything*)* and I'm able to overwhelm my negativity with a jolt of positive reinforcement. The same thing works in poker.

Try it and see. Next time you've made a tragic blunder at the poker table, don't dwell on the mistake. Instead, remind yourself of some aspect of your life where you experience achievement, triumph, success. This will help you leave the error behind and return to your good, stable, *right mind* game.

Avoid bad neighborhoods (2). A college basketball player named Len Bias went number two in the 1986 NBA draft and died within days of a cocaine overdose. I have often speculated that Bias was thrilled about being the number two pick—but somehow not as thrilled as he felt he should have been; so he reinforced his buzz with cocaine, trying somehow to reach the level of ecstasy he supposed he was supposed to feel. I think about this when I book a tournament win and find myself asking, *Okay, now what?* Coming off a tournament high, I'm wired and pumped and happy and proud, and I'm strongly tempted to jump into a cash game, just to keep the high alive. Though the punishment for this mistake wouldn't be as severe for me as it was for Bias, I'd still be making my choice based on how I feel—how I want to *keep on feeling*—rather than on what's best for my poker and my bankroll. The sensible thing to do is to enjoy the victory and not try to make more of it than it is.

One could argue that coming off a tournament win, we're likely to be in a good *game frame* (a positive and productive state of mind) and could reasonably hope to parlay our tournament success into still more success in live action. This may be the case; however, you have to know for sure that you're jumping into that ring game to maximize your current edge, not to stretch the buzz. Remember: Focus on how you do, not on how you feel. This is the path to right mind.

MUDDY ROAD

True story: I'm playing in a no-limit hold'em tournament, and it's down to three short-handed tables. We're all in the money, so at least that pressure is off, but unfortunately I have put a different sort of pressure on myself by letting it be known that I'm "that *Killer Poker* guy." Sometimes this is good for my image, especially in the end stages of a tournament where the fact of my having made it to the money suggests that, as a poker author and self-described maven, I'm not entirely without a clue. Still, eyes are on me, and I feel like it's incumbent upon me to play correctly, for the sake of appearances and my reputation and all. We don't have to dwell upon how nonsensical this thinking is; I've made my bed and now find myself lying in it.

The blinds are $1000 and $2000, with antes of $500. We're seven-handed at this table, so 13 500-dollar chips go in the pot before the deal. I'm in the big blind, short-stacked, with only 15 chips left after having posted the blind. It's folded around to the button, who, with plenty of chips, makes the odd bet of $5500—11 chips. The small blind folds and now it's on me. Even though I'm holding only 6-9 offsuit, with 24 chips in the pot I think I have to call. If I do, I'll be getting better than a 3-1 return on my seven-chip investment, and what kind of hand is my opponent likely to have here? If he's got a big pair, then I'm in serious trouble, because he'll win in the neighborhood of 85 percent of the time. However, I'm only a 2-1 underdog to hands as good as A-K suited, and with

(A) Him on the button
(B) It being a short-handed game
(C) Us all in the money, and
(D) Me short-stacked

I can easily put him on a hand as weak as two unsuited big cards. It was a funny bet, though . . . 11 chips, a trap bet if I ever saw one. And do I stop to think about the possibility that I'm being sucked in by a big pair? Honestly, no. That thought never crossed my mind. All I can think about, dwell upon, obsess over, is how *stupid* I'm going to look, in the eyes of people who don't see the odds the same way I do, when I turn over that 6-9 offsuit. I am *so* not playing proper poker at this moment. I know, I know . . . *play right now!* It's like I've never even *read* one of my books, much less written them. Still, I think it's right to call, so I'm going to call, and public perception be damned!

But that's not the stupid part.

Here comes the stupid part.

I toss in seven chips, *and then turn over my cards!*

That's right, I was so concerned about how bad I was about to look, I forgot that I wasn't all in. Whoo boy, how bad do you think I look now?

Well, the predictable cry goes up from players and rail-birds alike. The tournament director comes over to make a ruling. This could be bad: If she thinks I revealed my cards to influence action, she can, at her discretion, kill my hand and give me a 20-minute penalty, which will kill me in the tournament, too. She decides, however, that I'm guilty of nothing worse than felony foolishness, and rules that my hand is live and my foe can exploit knowledge of my holding as he sees fit.

Mister Killer Poker Guy indeed!

Well, what do I need on the flop? A piece at least. A pair or two pair would be good. How about a straight draw? How about . . .

7♣-8♦-T♥ . . .

Oh, my. I flopped a straight. Boy, howdy.

Well, I push in my last eight chips. Can you believe it?

My opponent declines to call. So I don't get maximum value out of my hand, but at least I'm still alive in the tournament. My reputation, of course, is dead as disco.

And of course I feel like an idiot. My face is red, my palms are sweating, and I sense that the whole world, or at least the players at my table and some two dozen railbirds, are all mentally mocking me. Remorse and regret wash over me, which remorse and regret punish me on the very next hand when I fold in the face of a raise, even though the odds once again justified a call. Why did I fold? Because I couldn't stand to look so stupid again so soon.

I was living in the past.

I was *stuck* in the past.

Mired in torment over recent stupidity.

I had to let that go.

At that moment, Tanzan came to my rescue.

Tanzan was a 19th-century Japanese Buddhist monk and professor of philosophy at the Imperial University. His wisdom comes down to us today in the form of the following Zen story or *koan*.

Tanzan and Ekido were walking together down a muddy road in the rain. Coming around a bend in the road, they arrived at a small, swift stream, where a lovely young girl in full dress kimono stood crying.

"Why are you crying?" asked Tanzan.

In between tears, the girl explained that she was due at a wedding in a village on the far side of the stream, but to cross the stream meant to ruin her kimono and, needless to say, her entrance.

"Come on, girl," said Tanzan. With that, he hoisted the girl on his back, waded across the stream, and deposited

her on the far side, high, dry, and happy. She went off to the wedding, there presumably to catch the bouquet and/or get drunk. Tanzan and Ekido continued on down the road.

Ekido held his tongue until that night when they reached a lodging temple. Then he could no longer restrain himself. "We monks don't go near women," he told Tanzan, "especially not young and lovely ones. Our order forbids it. Yet you carried that girl across the stream. Why did you carry that girl?"

"I left the girl at the stream," replied Tanzan. "Why do you carry her still?"

"Why do you carry her still?"

I had made a mistake, a boneheaded blunder in full public view. I was in pain and, worse, I was *carrying* that pain. I had to let it go. Thanks to Tanzan, I had a strategy for doing so. I imagined myself standing at that stream, and I *put that girl down.* Sure, I had made a mistake, but the universe had bailed me out. Maybe God truly does protect fools and Mister Killer Poker Guys. In any event, my ass had been saved by profound luck, but I was still in danger, and would remain in danger as long as I allowed remorse and regret to warp my play. I put the girl down.

This is what Tanzan tells us to do. Put the girl down.

You flop top pair, top kicker, and drive hard against a solo opponent, who hits a two-outer to beat you. You commence to harangue your foe, ruining your peace, your patience, and your play.

Put the girl down!

After hours of dreary jackthrees, you flop a set, only to be run down by set-over-set, setting you up for an all-night pity party.

Why do you carry her still?

You walk away from a table one hand before the jackpot hits, and curse your rotten luck for days.

Let it go!

Can you think of any other situations where you have suffered bad luck, bad beats, or bad outcomes and then made the bad situation worse by holding on to negative feelings? Can you describe such a situation? Can you name the feelings? What did you do (or could you have done) to get well?

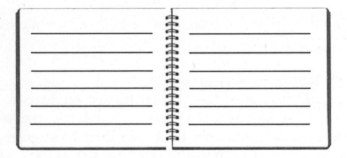

By the way, you may wonder if I ended up winning the tournament. Of course I did. With dumb luck like that on my side, how could I possibly not?

QUIT WINNERS

When someone asks you how you fared in a poker game, what kind of answer do you give them? Do you tell them the exact truth, an approximate truth, or do you lie? How does answering that question make you feel? Spend a moment to describe those feelings here.

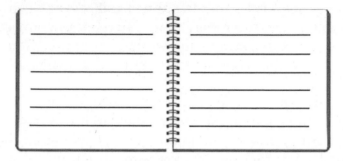

If you won and get to tell people you won, you probably feel good. If you lost and have to tell people you lost, you probably feel bad. What if you never had to tell them you lost? Wouldn't you spend more time feeling good? Well, yes you would, but since some losses are unavoidable, at least part of the time you would have to *lie*. Which is exactly the bold strategy I'm proposing here: Next time—any time—anyone asks you how you did playing hold'em, tell them you quit winners, because if you always tell everyone you quit winners, you never have to worry about how to tell anyone how you did.

Is this really an issue? Do other people's expectations of you and your poker outcomes really affect your poker performance? Well, let's take a look. We'll start by dividing the universe of people you know into those who play poker and those who don't play poker.

Among the people you know who play poker, we can further divide them into the categories of friend, foe, or irrelevant stranger. Why would you want to tell a friend you quit winners, even if you lost? Presumably because your friend understands what you're up to. He knows that you're trying to detach from outcomes. As your sympathetic poker-playing friend, he understands that the voracious need to *book a win* can put even the steadiest of players on tilt, and send them hurling rack after rack of chips into the bottomless pit of *gotta get even*. Your friend will realize that when you *say* you quit winners every time, you're merely protecting yourself from the *need* to quit winners every time. You and your friend thus conspire together to render the question irrelevant.

Now then, what if it's a foe, a poker-playing rival of yours, who comes up to you in the parking lot and says, "So, cowboy, how'd you do tonight?" Do you want to tell him you lost tonight? Do you want to tell him you lost *ever*? Why would you? Why would you want him to think that you're anything but an invincible hammer of hold'em? Tomorrow or the next day you may be up against him in a game. If he thinks you're coming off a loss, he'll try to pin another one on you. He'll imagine that you're vulnerable, fragile, friable—ready to lose again. So instead you tell him you quit winners, all the time and every time, as your standard pat answer. He may think you're lying, but so what? He is, as we've already established, no friend of yours. You don't owe him an honest accounting, and you will only surrender strategic advantage if you give it. Every time he asks how you did, you tell him you quit winners. From this he can only conclude that you always quit winners (at least when he happens to ask), or that you're savvy enough to say you did when you didn't. Either way you win.

As for random irrelevant strangers who ask how you did, who cares what they think? I'm not saying you should objectify all your fellow human beings, or even all your fellow players, but there's something much more crucial at stake, and that's the way you view yourself. If you've just absorbed a big loss and you have to *be honest* and tell everyone about it, how do you think that will make you feel? That's right: diminished and miserable; weak, impotent, glum. Who wants that sad self-image rattling around in their head? Tell 'em you quit winners. Remember, a useful fiction may be a fiction, but useful just the same. Telling strangers you quit winners perpetuates a useful fiction: It helps you see yourself as a winner. This breeds confidence. With enhanced confidence comes enhanced performance, and enhanced performance increases the likelihood that you'll quit winners next time for real.

There's a larger concept involved here, one having to do with the overall image you project to the world. You already understand that a negative consequence of telling bad beat stories is how it makes you look like a guy who gets beaten. Likewise, a player who goes around telling other players that he lost will inevitably come to be seen as a loser. However, a player who always says he wins whether it's true or not soon acquires a patina of positivity. Act like a winner all the time. You will seem like a winner whether you happened to quit winners today or not.

Now we come to the people in your life who don't play poker. These we divide into subcategories of those who view poker with a sympathetic eye and those who fricking don't. Those who view poker with a sympathetic eye genuinely want you to win, and genuinely feel badly for you when you don't. But they may not understand that losing sessions are inevitable. For the sake of saving them the pain of dealing with your loss, you may find yourself struggling to turn a losing session into a winning one, just so you can later tell loved ones or friends that you booked a win this time, and have it be the truth. This seems to me like the cat who hunts all night for a mouse that she can drop, dead, on her master's doorstep. It's fine when it works, but *what if you catch no mouse?*

Tell 'em you quit winners every time. Furthermore, tell them that you will tell them this every time, whether you quit winners or not, and explain your reasons why. Let them join you, just like your poker-playing allies join you, in your quest to detach from outcome. In this way you remove the pressure of their well-intended expectations, which leaves you free to concentrate on playing your best game, regardless of how the tally turns out.

Sadly, some people in your life may actually want you to lose. Can you believe it? Do you accept it? Does it cross your mind (or is it a fact already known to you) that there are people in your life who view your poker playing as degenerate behavior? They may give you overt support but covertly root for you to lose, just to reinforce for themselves their cherished beliefs that *gambling is bad* and *gamblers get punished*. If there are such people in your life and you can get them *out* of your life, I would certainly encourage you to do so, for they're toxic and negative and wrongheaded and who needs that? Then again, it may not be possible for you to get them out of your life. They may be relatives or in-laws or co-workers or otherwise affined to you, and you may be stuck with them and their negative opinion of the hold'em you hold dear. For these people especially, I suggest that you always tell 'em you quit winners and never care if they don't believe you. That way their negative opinion is *their* problem, not *your* problem, and you can carry on with your game.

If you don't care for the phrase "I quit winners," use one of your own coinage. What other positive (or neutral) statement could you give to anyone who asks how it recently went?

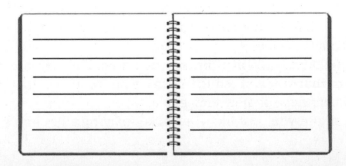

You may take a jaundiced view of this whole train of thought. It may strike you that I'm advocating lying to people in your life, players and non-players alike, and how can that be good? It can only be good, I reckon, if it serves a higher cause—that of helping you be a winning player more of the time. I put it to you that you simply can't play your best if you're worried about having to hold your losses up to the inspection of others, whether they have your best interests at heart or not. So keep that information to yourself. Tell them you quit winners. You'll feel better, and probably, so will they.

Then again, you may have spotted this pitfall: If you get into the habit of lying to others about your outcomes, what's to keep you from lying to you? If you're not responsible to your buddy/mentor/lover/spouse/dog for your outcomes, why should you be responsible to yourself? What's to keep the *useful fiction* that you always quit winners from turning into the *fantasy* or the *cherished belief* that you always quit winners, to the detriment of your game?

Nothing.

Nothing, that is, but your own honesty, and your own meticulous and detailed proof of performance. I won't go into the subject of record-keeping here, for I've dealt with it at length in my other books. I would just reiterate what we all know to be true: If you're not keeping full and complete records about your wins and losses, you're not serious about your game.

If you tell yourself the truth about your outcomes, it really doesn't matter what you tell others. You will have informed the only person who matters. Everything else is just propaganda, information that you deliver for psychological or situational reasons in service of the goal of quitting winners every chance you get.

2

♣ ♠ ♦ ♥

SITUATIONS

♧ ♤ ♢ ♡

Some hold'em situations are just completely cut and dried. If you're drawing to an inside straight, you have no more than four outs no matter how you do the math. Other situations are not so clear. When the player to your left grabs chips just as you start to bet, does he intend to call or is he falsely telegraphing that intent in an effort to make you check? The answer lies not in pure math, but in an impure understanding of that player, his capabilities, mindset, past performance, mood, and other considerations.

Still other situations that should be black and white end up getting colored by our desires, fears, prejudices, or other perceptual warps. During lapses in self-control, I have certainly found myself on a flush draw heads up against some arrogant airhole I couldn't stand. I knew I had to hit to win, and I also knew that the pot wasn't offering sufficient ROI (return on investment) to justify my call, yet I called just the same. I wanted that rat bastard to *lose*, and this desire caused me to view a folding situation as a calling one instead.

Has that ever happened to you? I'll bet it has; that or something like it. In the spirit of candor, I invite you to recall and record such an incident now. Don't be afraid of telling yourself the truth. No one's looking over your shoulder, and you won't be graded on the outcome.

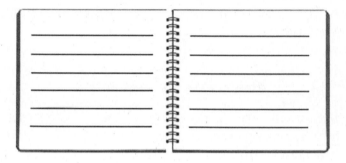

I've said it before: In poker as in life, what you see depends on where you stand. It would be great if things were otherwise, but they're not. It would be terrific if we could analyze every hold'em situation from a perfectly neutral point of view, but the very phrase "point of view" suggests that there's no such thing as neutral. Bias exists; unacknowledged bias leeches poison into the groundwater of our thinking.

So as you ponder the following situations, consider that it's possible to know the right course and still take the wrong action. Everyone makes mistakes; the biggest mistake, it seems to me, is pretending you never do.

Remember also that any analysis of any hold'em situation must necessarily be incomplete because it's impossible to list all the relevant details and variables. We might wonder, for instance, how to play A-J preflop in late position in the face of a raise, a reraise and two calls, but we can't hope to know for sure without knowing the overall tenor and makeup of the game. In a tight game against disciplined foes, you might consider your A-J dominated and fold. But if the game is a clueless parade, where people will make or take major heat with stepchild holdings, you may be good for a call or a raise. Use these situations, then, not to reach definitive answers but to sharpen your analytical skills and to fortify your own sense of self. Think, in other words, about how you think. There's tremendous potential for growth in that.

PRE-GAME FESTIVITIES

We'll start our investigation by examining some situations we face before we even sit down to play. These situations, and the choices they force us to make, can impact our overall success far more than how we play pocket aces. After all, we only see pocket aces once every 221 hands, but we're present at that table in that club and that game or tournament for every hand—hand after hand after hand.

Two of Clubs

You live in a town with two cardrooms of equal size. This weekend, one room is hosting a major tournament that promises to attract a lot of out-of-town traffic. The side-game action should be excellent. The other club has nothing special on offer, just the usual gang sitting around playing the usual games. You're not interested in tournament play today, but you do want to make the most of the fact that the circus is in town. Where should you play and why?

COMMENT: There are two ways of looking at this question—both wrong. Let's see why.

If we go to the tournament club, we assume that we'll find a lot of games at a lot of limits, a whole happening poker scene where, presumably, we'll encounter players in all stages of tiredness and weakness. We might see an opportunity in waiting until players bust out of the various tournaments, and, in their anger and frustration, jump into live games where, one would hope, we can pounce on them, exploit their anger and frustration, and take their money home. Then again, these are tournament players who have come from out of town to be here. In a world of poker Darwinism, they must have at least some skills or they wouldn't be here in the first place. We might find that our plan to "feast on the bustouts" merely brings us head to head with players who are out of the tournament, yeah, but not out of ability or smarts.

If we go to the other club, we expect to find that attendance is way down over there, because some of the regular crew are across town trying to make the most of the big tournament. Those players who remain, we might conclude (or hope), are in a sense the bottom of some barrel: players too weak or underfunded or uninspired to get involved with the tournament scene. But they're so few in number, and so poorly heeled, that there's really not much money to be won here now. Or so we might speculate.

And that's the key word: *speculate.*

We speculate that busted, steaming tournament players present us with a target of opportunity. Or we speculate that players who can't or won't play tournaments will yield up their dough on demand. We speculate . . . but we do not know.

So . . . go know.

Go to both clubs. Look in on all the games. Find the ones that offer favorable conditions, regardless of *why* or *how* those conditions emerged. In other words:

> Don't speculate, investigate.

Can you do that? Are you willing to make the effort, and if not, why not? Would you rather rely on untested assumptions, or are you just not that motivated to win money? Based on past experience (the place was jamming last year) you might be able to predict where favorable opportunities lie, but you won't *know* until you investigate.

Game Versus Game

You're on the sign-up list for two hold'em games, one at $10–$20 and the other at $15–$30. You have the bankroll and the mindset to play in either game, and while waiting for your name to be called, you give them both a good, hard look. Average stack size in the $10–$20 game is under $500. During the short time you watch, you see four or five callers per hand, with almost no preflop raises. The overall shape of the game is loose, passive, and straightforward. In the $15–$30 game, the average stack size is around $1500, and at least three players have five racks (of 5-dollar chips) apiece. Almost every hand is raised before the flop, and check-raises and reraises are rampant throughout the play of hands.

A seat becomes available in the $15–$30 game. You think it'll be another 15 or 20 minutes before you can get into the $10–$20 game. What should you do?

A) Join the $15–$30 game and do your best to beat it.
B) Plan to play snug in the $15–$30 game and move to the $10–$20 game at the first opportunity.
C) Decline the seat in the $15–$30 game and continue to railbird the $10–$20 game.

COMMENT: Based on the available information, the $10–$20 game is clearly the softer target. With average stack sizes below $500, you can buy in for one rack and be a top dog. Better still, buy in for two racks and seize the role of chip bully. Over in the $15–$30 game, you'll need three racks just to have an average chip position. While you certainly don't mind putting that kind of money in play, you can reasonably predict that with three players running hot enough, or playing well enough, to accumulate five racks apiece, you'll take heat from inspired, aggressive players from the moment you sit down. Even if you intend to stay in the game only until your $10–$20 seat comes open, you'll be giving away a lot of edge by taking a shot at this game.

You should wait. The question is: *Can* you wait? Do you have the patience to decline a seat in a tough game in favor of a later, more favorable situation? Here's where desire starts to color perception. You've come to the club to play poker, after all. If your need for action is sufficiently great, you might just convince yourself that you've got a workable short-term strategy to survive in the $15–$30 game before settling in at the $10–$20 game for the night. You might rationalize participating by promising yourself to play only premium hands and folding everything else. The fly in that particular ointment is *you need to hit to win.* If you don't get lucky and catch some cards, you'll just fold all your hands, and sacrifice two or three rounds of big and small blinds while waiting (patiently!) for your other seat to open. You'll be paying good money just to mark time. A cup of coffee and a bear claw would be cheaper.

And that's not even the worst case. In the worst case, your discipline cracks, you take a flier on a couple of hands that don't hit, let yourself get pushed off a pot or two by the well-funded and inspired big stacks, and find yourself half a rack back before you finally move, tail between your legs, to the $10–$20 game.

I'm not saying that hit-and-run won't work or can't work. I'm just saying that it should be employed as a *strategy*, not an *excuse*. If you think the game is beatable, beat it. If you don't think it's beatable, find a magazine and a quiet corner and *relax*.

Game selection is critical; this we know. But it's not enough to analyze the various games you're thinking of joining. You also have to analyze yourself and be certain that you're joining the right game for the right reason. You want to draw good conclusions—and then act on the conclusions you draw. There's nothing so seductive as *the first open seat*. Learn to say no to unfavorable tables and you'll always sit down in a position to win.

Rebuy Rebus

There's a hold'em tournament tonight at Club Succubus and Incubus. The buy-in is $120, with unlimited 100-dollar rebuys and a single 100-dollar add-on. There figures to be a large field of competitors, many of whom are, in your estimation, "dead money walking." The house is guaranteeing a prize pool of $30,000, plus every entrant gets a really nice hat. You like hats. You like tournaments. You like your chances in this event. The only thing you don't like is the prospect of catching *rebuy fever,* a disease that has afflicted you before. In fact, even one or two rebuys is more than you feel you can comfortably invest tonight, and satellites, alas, are not an available option. What should you do?

A) Buy in, but plan not to rebuy or add on.
B) Buy in, and plan to make the add-on only.
C) Spend as much as you need to, and bankroll be damned.
D) Skip it.

COMMENT: There are a lot of extrinsic factors to consider here, including the size and quality of the field, the fact of the guaranteed minimum prize pool, and the really nice hat. But these extrinsic figures pale to insignificance in relation to this one *intrinsic* question: How do you feel going in? Your state of mind will skew your decision-making process here, and three times out of four it'll lead you down a wrong road.

Suppose you decide to enter the tournament, but not to rebuy or add on. You're good for one shot, you figure, and if you bust out, well, so be it. This plan yields significant edge to your more profligate foes. Knowing that they can't go broke till the rebuy period ends, they'll play the early rounds with a confidence you won't have. Also, if they add on and you don't, they'll enter the post-rebuy period better equipped for combat. Overall, this scheme will only work for you if you play well enough (or get lucky enough) to never need a rebuy and also to emerge from the first round of play with *so many chips* that adding on wouldn't materially improve your position. This can happen, but it's rare, and especially so when your unwillingness to rebuy has tied a hand behind your back during the first phase of play.

Hamstrung by false economy, then, you can't seriously hope to contend for a tournament win. About the only way you could make this situation worse for yourself would be to reveal this plan to your foes. The combined force of their unlimited rebuys would crack you like an egg.

Okay, that won't work, so how about this? You commit $220 to the tournament. You'll play ultra-conservative to survive the first rounds of play, take the add-on when it comes, and then go to war after the rebuy period ends. An extreme execution of this strategy has you actually staying away from the table until the rebuy period ends. Sure, you'll pay some blinds, but not enough to break you, and you'll never put yourself at risk for that dreaded unwanted rebuy. Of course you also won't put yourself in a position to accumulate chips, and even with the add-on you'll enter the post-rebuy period with a mediocre stack. This seems to violate the first law of Killer Poker: *go big or go home*. If you truly only have $220 to invest, hunt up a lower buy-in tournament where your limited resources will stretch further.

Option three has you going hell-for-leather, playing a wide-open, aggressive game and taking whatever rebuys the situation requires, plus, of course, the add-on. This is close to proper rebuy strategy, but it's not a strategy you can execute well. Why? Because you're *scared*. You told yourself going in that you didn't want to put four, five, six hundred bucks into this tournament. If you find yourself doing just that, it will have a predictable negative impact on your confidence, your discipline, your self-image, and your overall performance. In the worst case, you'll reach a *nose is open* state, where you're bleeding rebuys beyond count and past caring. You may even end up in a tournament underlay situation. Then, even when you win you lose.

(What's a tournament underlay? Suppose ten contenders put up ten bucks each for a winner-take-all prize of $100. All other things being equal, the winning chance for each contender is 1 in 10, and the payoff is exactly matched to the odds at 9 to 1—risk $10 to win $90. If Spendy Pete puts in $20 instead of $10, his return on investment is cut in half. He's still a 9 to 1 underdog, but now he's risking $20 to win the same $90, for a payout of only 4.5 to 1. He is now underlaying the field. This is why it's important not to make rebuys far beyond the field's average, since each rebuy above the average decreases your relative ROI.)

Which brings us to the final option: *Skip it*. You hate this option and so do I because we want action, *tournament* action, and it's happening here and it's happening now, tonight, right in front of our pressed-against-the-candy-store-window faces. Too bad for us that it's happening at a cost we find uncomfortable. But that's reality, and all of the other rebuy (so-called) strategies outlined above really only serve to deny reality. If we don't have the mental or financial resources to play a rebuy tournament correctly, we simply *must not play*.

This is not such a heinous choice. There are always other tournaments, rebuy and non-rebuy alike, at all levels of investment. Stay within your comfort level, so that you can play your best game without sweating or fretting the consequences of going broke.

This begs the question of what, exactly, is proper rebuy strategy for a rebuy tournament? Conventional wisdom says (and while I often say that conventional wisdom is for conventional people, I'll go along with it here) that if there's one optional rebuy and/or add-on, you should plan to take it. For defensive purposes you almost have to, because most of the rest of the field will, and you don't want to give away that edge. Again, the exception would be if you've accumulated so many chips that adding on wouldn't add even so much as 20 percent to your stack. Conversely, if you have so few chips left that adding on would still leave you perilously short-stacked, you might consider investing your money elsewhere. But again, these are considerations based on the tournament situations, not any covert fear of losing money that you haven't yet rooted out and consciously addressed.

In unlimited rebuy tournaments the question gets trickier. First, map out in advance your worst-case scenario, and know how many rebuys you're willing to invest. Recognize that if you go into your pocket three or four times, you're going to start moving out ahead of the ROI curve (unless everyone else has rebuy fever, too). Recognize also that if you're rebuying that frequently, you're probably not play-ing your best game today. There's no shame in walking away from the table if you're not playing well. There's real shame in staying and throwing good rebuys after bad. Rule of thumb, then: If you're in control, playing well, and spending in proportion to the rest of the field, it's okay to rebuy as the situation demands. If it's not your night, say good night.

Seat Me, Seymour

You're called to a $20–$40 hold'em game. There are two seats open, and they're both available to you. Looking around the table, here's what you see:

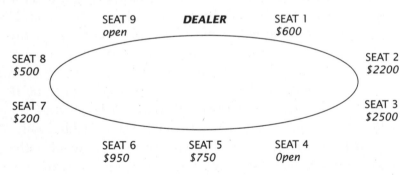

| SEAT 9 | DEALER | SEAT 1 |
| open | | $600 |

SEAT 8
$500

SEAT 2
$2200

SEAT 7
$200

SEAT 3
$2500

| SEAT 6 | SEAT 5 | SEAT 4 |
| $950 | $750 | Open |

Given that you don't know anything about the players but their stack size, which open seat would you choose, and why?

COMMENT: Years ago, groundbreaking poker author and theorist Mike Caro noted that money tended to flow clockwise around a poker table. He pointed out that, absent significant skill differential, positional advantage would keep the money moving. For this reason alone, you'd want to grab seat four, just to be downstream from the highest concentration of wealth. But there's a much more important reason for taking seat four, not nine, and it has nothing to do with being able to gaze directly into the dealer's baleful eyes.

The distribution of money at this table tells us that the game is currently being dominated by seats two and three. We don't know whether they're playing well or just catching cards, but either way they're the forces to be reckoned with here. If nothing else, their mounds of chips tell us that they have sufficient ammunition to play aggressively, if they so choose. If we take seat nine, these monster stacks will get to act after us, and make the most of their positional advantage. If we slide into seat four, on the other hand, they have to act before we do, and when we do go up against them (in an earnest effort to relieve them of their surplus wealth) we'll have the benefit of acting after they do. So, then, all other things being equal . . .

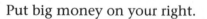

Put big money on your right.

This strategy is not without pitfalls. Looking again at the table layout, we see that one or another of those big stacks will have the button every time we take the big blind or the small blind. It's no happy happenstance to have big-money-plus-best-position attacking our blinds every lap around the table, but that's a natural tradeoff we must make when we attempt to gain positional advantage over well-heeled players. Perhaps your best positional advantage would be in another game altogether. Failing that, and until new information about the players gives you a better sense of where to sit, put the big money on your right where you can keep a weather eye on it and stay out of its way if you have to.

FIRE IN THE HOLE CARDS

Many hold'em hole card decisions are automatic. Any player who gets past the elementary stage of "any two will do" quickly learns that big pairs play best against few opponents and big draws play best against many. This section assumes that you know your basic starting requirements—but encourages to you speculate once more on those times when knowing and acting are two different things.

Bottled Rockets

You're running bad. It's been a nightmare of missed draws, second-best hands, and heinous suckouts. Your image is shredded; it seems like every time you enter the pot the others just pile on. Wallowing in your misery, you now find yourself holding pocket aces under the gun. Assuming that you're not so despondent as to fold, should you call, raise, or call hoping to reraise?

COMMENT: Many players in this situation, feeling snakebit like they are, will want to slow-play their aces. This is wrong on the face of it, but it's even worse because they have two contradictory reasons for doing so. On one hand, feeling snakebit, they want to minimize their loss in case their aces don't hold up. On the other hand, they're in a deep hole and imagine that a big volume multi-way win will get them well in a hurry in case their aces *do* hold up. In any event, their thinking is tainted by their feeling, and so their actions—*whatever* actions—are fundamentally misguided.

Let's review some basic math. A-A is a big favorite against any single random hand (about 3.5 to 1 over J-T suited to a suit other than the aces; about 8 to 1 over 7-2 offsuited in suits counterfeit to the aces). But A-A will win only one time in three or four against a field of six random hands. The math is immutable: If you don't raise with pocket aces and let a lot of limpers limp in, you're giving yourself the worst of it.

What about calling with the hope of reraising? After all, if your image is that tattered, can't someone downstream be expected to throw in a raise, just to kick you when you're down? Well, suppose they do. Suppose you call under the gun and a couple of middle position players call also. The betting swings around to the cutoff seat, who obligingly raises. The button and the big blind like their hands for two bets, then you make it three. In-for-a-penny-in-for-a-pound thinking then takes over, and you find yourself in a capped pot (good!) against five foes (bad!).

With aces it's simple: Your chances of winning are inversely proportional to the number of people in the pot.

Raise up front.
Raise to narrow the field.
Raise.

Sad fact: Sometimes we don't get maximum value from aces. Sometimes we raise preflop and win only the blinds. This makes us feel cheated somehow; those aces are so damn rare, we feel we deserve more from them when we get them—especially when we're running bad! Swallow this bitter pill. Raise with your aces. Where I come from, there's a saying, "Slow-play aces, go to hell—usually right away."

Blind Man's Fluff

You're in the big blind with A-K offsuit. A diehard blind stealer, capable of raising with anything from middle pairs or J-T suited on up, raises from late position. The button and the small blind call. It's back to you. What action do you take, and why?

COMMENT: Of course you're not going to fold, so the question is, should you raise or flat-call? Raising seems like an attractive option because big slick is a big hand. It figures to be a favorite over the blind-stealer, who could have any medium-strength hand, and also over the other callers, who'd have three-bet with a big pair. The trouble is, while big slick is a big hand, it doesn't play well up front with its naked strength revealed. If you three-bet from the big blind, it's like waving your hand and announcing, "Hey, powerhouse here!" Attentive opponents will take note of this, and ask themselves what kind of powerhouse you might have. Since you're more likely to have unpaired big cards than a big pair, they're more likely to put you on exactly the hand you have.

Now here comes the flop, and it's either good for your hand or it's not. If it's good for your hand, rich in aces or kings, everyone knows it and they can get out of your way. If it's not good for your hand, everyone knows that too, and now they can start to monkey around with you. Had you flat-called with your A-K, no one could define your hand more narrowly than to say, "Well it's probably not total trash, or he'd have folded." Any ace or king on the flop would then give you power *plus deception,* and open the door to all sorts of fruitful check-raise scenarios.

You may have heard that A-K plays well against fewer opponents, and this is true, but it's not an argument for raising here. Do you expect the blind-stealer to suddenly get religion and muck his hand? He thinks you're just pissed at him for raising. And the other callers? Having called two bets, they're highly unlikely to let their hands go. Your attempt to winnow the competition merely alerts the competition that you have a hand you want to winnow with.

Here's what I suggest: Save your big blind reraises for A-A, K-K . . . *or total bluffs!* You can reraise with top pairs because the hands are so strong it doesn't matter that they're well defined. You can also reraise on a bluff with middling cards because you have precisely *misdefined* your hand with your raise. Now if the flop comes with an ace or a king, your clever opponents can get away from the hand and commend themselves for not getting trapped by your (presumed) big hand. And if the flop hits your highly disguised holding, why, then you can trap them for real.

To reiterate, the problem with raising with A-K in this situation is that it's not strong enough to dominate all by itself, and yet it reveals its naked strength to the field. Big hand does not always mean big raise, especially in the big blind.

New Blood, Fresh Meat

It's a $20–$40 game and you have the button. The blinds are both weak-tight. A new player, someone you don't know, has just joined the game on your immediate right, and posted $20. It's folded around to the newster, who checks. Now it's on you. You hold 6-T offsuit. You're pretty sure a raise will drop the blinds. What should you do?

A) Fold.
B) Call.
C) Raise.

COMMENT: As a Killer Poker player, I just love a raise right here. I may be out of line with my 6-T offsuit, but to tell the truth I'd take the same action with almost any cards. The purpose of this raise is not just to win the pot, but also to define the new foe. The truth is revealed under pressure, so I'm going to apply some here. Many players fear this sort of attack. They enter a game in a slightly agitated state. Their adrenaline is starting to flow and they're facing a table filled with strangers . . . enemies . . . threats. They feel that everyone is checking them out, taking their measure. They don't want to send the message *I can be bullied,* and would dearly love to get through their forced post without facing preflop pressure. Deny that desire! Start right away to put them off their play.

Suppose you raise and your foe reraises. Do you throw your hand away? Not necessarily. Bets send messages, and his reraise may mean nothing more than *don't dick around with me!* Raise him back. Close out the betting. If you get a favorable flop, attack again; if not, try to get to the river as cheaply as possible. Remember, you're setting this foe up for the entire session to come. You want to know what he's made of, and the first hand is as good a time as any to find out.

A second choice would be to fold (your admittedly crappy hand) and do your learning at someone else's expense. But can the small blind or the big blind be counted on to step up? The last thing you want is to let a new player get comfortable in the game. If you fold here (or, worse yet, call) you're allowing him to feel at home, and that's bad for your long-term prospects.

But what about your short-term prospects? After all, 6-T offsuit is hardly a hand to go to war with.

Or is it?

Granted, 6-T offsuit is a big dog to big pairs—but how often is your foe likely to walk into a big pair in this situation? Pocket pairs come along once every 17 hands; big pocket pairs (ten through ace) less than half that often. Thus, he's got a roughly 3 percent chance of having a dominant pair here. *Three percent!* If he's a straightforward player and he chooses to defend his post, he's much more likely to be in there with unpaired big cards than with a big pair.

How big an edge does he have with, say, A-J offsuit? About 2 to 1. But check it out: Counting the dead blind money in the pot (assuming the blinds will fold) you're getting approximately correct odds for your meager 6-T offsuit ... *and he might fold!*

If he doesn't fold, you still have position.

If he's terribly clever, he might play back at you.

But he's not likely to play back at you. He's a new player. He's just getting his feet wet. He's probably warned himself against playing too loose or getting too crazy before he gets used to the table and his foes. That's why we say ...

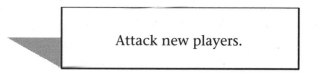

Attack new players.

Hit them first and hit them fast. Find out what they're made of. Remember, you can divide your opponents broadly into two categories: those who *think;* and those who *feel.* Those who *think* will see your gambit for what it is—a gambit. They will respond in kind, defining themselves for you as skillful, savvy players who must be treated with respect. Those who *feel* will see your raise as an unsportsmanlike annoyance and a threat. Their emotional response will define them as emotional players who can, over the course of the session, be skinned, turned inside out, and left hanging on the shed.

Little Big Pair

At an eight-handed table full of very tight, very predictable players, you're in middle position with pocket tens. Surrounded as you are by the tighty-frighties, you mentally prepare yourself to fire off a raise. But, surprise . . . before the action gets to you there's a raise, a re-raise, and a call. Now it's on you. Do you

    A) Call it.
    B) Cap it.
    C) Cast it out.

Bonus question: How does your decision make you feel?

COMMENT: Most players will come to the right conclusion that this hand needs to be mucked—and many will feel ever-so-slightly resentful at having to give up on a good pair. Those who feel sufficiently resentful will call or raise anyway—*take that!*—and pay the price for letting their emotions get the better of their evaluations.

Now then, why is this hand an easy fold? The players behind you are tight, so they can't be expected to enter the pot with much of anything inferior to your pocket tens. If they don't call, you can't count on getting the crowd you need to justify your 7.5-1 draw to a set. As for the players already in the pot, given that they're tight too, they're not in there with string cheese; no, you have to put them on big pairs or big paint.

There are only two ways this hand plays profitably from the flop forward. One way is to flop a ten, the aforementioned 7.5-1 shot, and hope it holds up. The other way is to see a flop with zero—*zero*—cards higher than a 9, in which case all you have to do is 1) come out swinging; 2) hope that all your foes are in there with unpaired overcards and not overpairs; 3) have them all run scared when you bet; and/or 4) hope no overcards hit the turn or the river. That's a hell of a parlay. Assuming that everyone behind you folds low cards and the three players left have high cards, your chances of catching your nine-high flop are only about 1 in 4—and everything still has to break perfect from there.

You know, I think I was wrong before when I said that most players will recognize this as a folding situation. Probably a third of us will discount, devalue, or ignore the raises, and imagine that our tens are legitimate contenders. Another third will know that we're dominated but throw our bets in anyhow, because, hey, we might just hit our set and then we can make it all back on (yum, yum) *implied odds*. The final third—or maybe sixth or sixteenth—of us will have the clarity and the fortitude to make this good laydown.

Much talk is made in hold'em circles about starting requirements. In many books and on many websites, even doctoral dissertations, you can find variously interpreted start charts that all boil down to the same thing: Play good cards and muck bad ones. But it's not as simple as that. Frail humans that we are, we're prone to making mistakes, and one of the worst mistakes we can make in hold'em is seeing our good hands as *something very special*. When we pick up big cards, we start to get stars in our eyes. We project ourselves into our immediate future and see those big cards turning into big pots, and big pots into big wins. With our perspective thus filtered through desire, we neglect or ignore or deny the rest of the field. It's not so much a question of knowing which hands to play and which to fold; it's much more a question of having the honesty and the equanimity to recognize that a good start does not guarantee a big finish, and that all the wishing in the world will not make it so.

We can talk ourselves into anything. We can. We might know the start charts by heart, but if we find ourselves on the button holding 3-4 offsuit and see a betting sequence of raise, reraise, cap, call, call, call, in a moment of weakness we might still find a way to convince ourselves to throw our bets in. Perhaps we'll rationalize it this way: *With all that enthusiastic raising and calling, all the big cards are out, and what's left in the deck are small cards—my cards! Why, I'm practically a lock to hit this flop!*

Sigh. Practically a lock.

And the flop is only the beginning.

Let's push on.

FLOP TILL YOU DROP

One of the reasons Texas hold'em has replaced seven-card stud as America's preferred poker game is what I call the economy of information. In seven-stud, it costs you a minimum of one bet to see four cards—57 percent of your total eventual seven. In hold'em, as little as one bet can get you a look at your hole cards plus the flop—71 percent of your final fit. No wonder there are so many flopheads out there. In games without a lot of preflop raising, that flop is really quite a bargain.

Or is it?

Bottom (Pair) Feeding

In a frenzy of Killer Poker aggressiveness, you've bullied your way into the pot with a late position raise and a holding of A♦-9♦. Both blinds and one limper have called, and the flop comes 9♣-K♦-J♠. Your foes are lemming types who will call preflop raises with middle pairs, draw to gutshot straights, and stick around with bad jacks or kings. In this case, they check around to you. It's a $10–$20 game with $80 in the pot. Do you check or bet, and why?

COMMENT: Much can be made of the fact that A♦-9♦

isn't really a raising hand to begin with, and that anyone who finds himself in this sort of post-flop mess pretty much deserves what he gets. Contrarian that I am, I beg to differ. In the first place, given the game situation (all those "it depends" variables), raising with A-9 suited might be a perfectly viable play. More to the point, people do make errors in judgment. They do get into holes, and then face the challenge of digging themselves out. The purpose of this example is to show that surrender is not the only option.

In most cases with this flop I'm going to have to improve to win, because in most cases my opponents will have holdings in the *wheelhouse*, also known as the playing zone; cards from ten on up. This means they've got at least gutshot straight draws and/or better pairs than mine. I'm going to bet anyhow, because while I'm vulnerable to overpairs, I may get calls from worse hands like middle pairs, and anyone drawing to a gutshot is drawing with the worst of it. Also, let's give everyone a chance to fold if they want.

If I don't bet the flop I'm declaring the pot an orphan pot, and the first person to bet on the turn can adopt it for free. If I *do* bet the flop, I retain control of the hand, and can check or bet the turn depending on what card comes.

In most cases I'd rather be the bettor than the caller, for the bettor has two ways to win: by improving, or by making everyone else fold. Therefore:

> All things being
> equal, be active.

On the micro level, checking this flop isn't a terrible play, but on the macro level it does nothing for your long-term goal of taking over the table. For this reason, if I have to err, I'm going to err on the side of action, rather than caution. In the worst case, I show down a losing hand, demonstrate my willingness to bet with the worst of it, and get paid off next time I actually have the goods.

Foreclosure Raise

Holding Big Maxx (K♣-Q♣), you catch a flush draw with a flop of T♣-8♣-4♥. You're first to act, with five players waiting behind. Do you

A) Bet.
B) Check-fold.
C) Check-call.
D) Check-raise.

COMMENT: Okay, you're 2-1 against making your flush, so you only need two callers here to make a profitable bet. But there's a better option, and that's to go for the foreclosure raise. Check. If everyone else checks, you've gotten a free card—not a bad thing here. If someone bets (and in a field this large, you can probably count on it), go ahead and raise. Maybe they'll put you on a draw, for the foreclosure raise is not exactly an unknown ploy. But suppose they do put you on a draw? Any Q, J, 9, 7, 6, or 5 could conceivably hit a straight draw—to say nothing of the clubs. With so many scary cards in the deck, your check-raise on the flop will set up a very threatening check on the turn. If you hit, you bet; if you miss, you hope for a free ride to the river.

Many players will only check-and-call their flush draw here, because they don't want to invest more money in the pot until they've got a sure thing. Trouble is, a club on the turn will greatly retard the growth of this pot. Now would be a good time to recall that *individual outcomes don't matter.* If you're betting with the best of it, it's immaterial whether you hit on this hand or not. If you've got a 2-1 shot and the pot is offering you 3-1 or more, you want to get as much money in as possible. You're betting with the best of it. Thus:

> If you have the best of it,
> don't fear the worst of it.

Not to put too fine a point on it, if you're too timid to bet, you're probably too timid to play. And if you're too timid to bet your draws, your foes will always know you're betting with a made hand.

Stealth Ace

Having picked up a pair of kings in middle position, you raised into a full field and ended up with five callers. The flop comes, 6♣-A♦-2♥. There's a bet and two calls before the action gets to you. Glancing downstream you see at least two other players giving off reliable call-tells. Should you

A) Raise to drive out the callers.
B) Call to suck in the callers.
C) Muck your hand.
D) Show your hand and then muck.

COMMENT: Many players in this situation are exactly half-smart. They're smart enough to know that mucking those kings is a good—in fact, a necessary—laydown. They're not, though, quite smart enough to disguise how smart they are. These flawed competitors, leading with their egos, betray a fatal compulsion to *show those kings* when they fold. They just *have* to let everyone know what a terrific, disciplined laydown they made.

In a word, hogwash.

Why would you *ever* want your opponents to know that you're capable of folding a big pair? So they can *admire* you? You don't want their admiration, you want their *money*, and educating them about your real abilities and discipline must necessarily have the opposite effect. So *show-and-tell* is absolutely the worst option here.

Calling and raising are pretty stenchy choices, too. With three players in the pot already, and more to come, you have to know that there's at least one ace out there against you. Probably more: You raised preflop, after all, so put at least some of your foes on quality hands. What else could everyone be in there with? Middle pairs? Draws to small inside straights? Maybe someone is on a steal (especially if you've demonstrated your capacity for "good" laydowns) but they can't *all* be out of line.

So fold. Of course, fold.

And yet, many don't. Many players will call in this situation. They look at that ace on board and . . . *just* . . . *don't* . . . *see* . . . *it* . . . *at* . . . *all.* I call this the phenomenon of the *stealth ace.* Certain players holding big pairs, notably pocket kings, actually become blind to an ace on the flop. It literally vanishes from view. We've already discussed the root of this blindness: Big pairs come along so rarely that they often come with an attendant sense of entitlement. Having been fortunate enough to start with a big hand, we believe that we're owed a big pot. This belief will cause certain weak-minded players to convince themselves that the ace is not a threat. Maybe they think no one is paired to the ace. Maybe they're investing in the dream of catching a king. *Why not? People catch two-outers all the time, don't they? Well, some of the time. Okay, in fact, rarely. Still, it is pocket kings. . . .* And so the circus comes to town.

It's not a bad circus if you're on the ace end of it. If you know that your opponent will get stuck on his kings, by all means hammer away with your ace. Just don't bother bluffing. You can't represent aces your foe can't see.

Simply put, then:

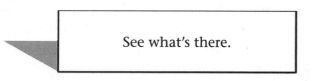

See what's there.

This would seem self-evident, yet an astounding number of poker players can't master this simple trick of perception. Don't you be one.

In Boss Command

Holding A-K, you have raised to isolate, and gotten heads-up against one foe. The flop comes A-3-7 rainbow. Your opponent bets. Should you fold, call, or raise?

COMMENT: Raise. Your opponent is highly unlikely to have a better hand than you have here. Maybe he got supremely lucky and flopped a set or A-little two pair, in which case you'll hear about it soon enough and can proceed with appropriate caution. It's much more likely, though, that he's betting with a worse ace than yours, trying to drive you off whatever miserable cheese he feels you had the effrontery to raise with in the first place. (Maybe he's a stealth ace victim here.) Don't get cute and just call. Get maximum value, for this is another case where your opponent's subjective reality can be used against him. Players holding lesser aces will find it very difficult to get away from this hand. If they do wake up and put you on a better ace, they'll start hoping to hit their kicker or they'll contrive to convince themselves that you're bluffing. Of course, you don't want to be bluffing in this situation; nor should you do so if you know that your opponent is capable of playing bad aces to begin with. Simply restrict yourself to good aces, push them hard, and make money on your foes' optimistic calls.

This would be a good time to remind ourselves about the *anyace line*. Hold'em games can be defined as existing either above or below the anyace line. In most low-limit and many mid-limit games, lots of players will call with hands containing an ace and any other card. A game where most people make this call is said to be below the anyace line. If you find yourself in such a game, make the two following adjustments: First, restrict your own play of aces to good ones; second, bet those aces aggressively, for they're big money makers in situations where they dominate.

Next time you play, be sure to note which of your foes will play bad aces. Bad aces make good targets.

TURN, TURN, TURN

Fixed-limit hold'em being what it is, the turn is where many players turn tail and run. They'll take a flier on anything on the flop because, what the heck, it's only one small bet, and they've still got two cards coming. These same players, though, will frequently deny themselves that second draw by folding on the turn for the price of a big bet. This is worth remembering: If you flop an open-ended straight draw, you're only about a 2-1 dog to make your straight between here and the river—but only if you *stay till the river.*

Your single draw on the turn is only a one-in-five shot. That's why you have to compute your odds bet by bet, or else commit yourself in advance to seeing all bets. Many players miscalculate their odds on the flop and cower out on the turn.

Strictly Odds

In a $10–$20 hold'em game, you got a free look from the big blind with 7-8 offsuit. You and five others saw a flop of 6-9-3 rainbow. You checked the flop and called a single bet behind a bettor and two other callers. The turn is a jack. You check. There's an early position bet and two calls before it gets back to you. Should you raise, fold, or call?

COMMENT: First, let's crunch the numbers. Six callers put $60 in the pot preflop. On the flop you found yourself facing a $10 call into a $90 pot, an easy call (so easy that you might also have raised) with eight outs to what figures to be the nut straight. Do you have a similarly easy call on the turn? Another $60 has gone into the pot, bringing the total to $160. Your $20 call into a $160 pot would give you an 8-1 ROI, while your chances of making your straight are roughly one in six, so you still have favorable pot odds. You also have implied odds, because if you hit your straight on the river, you'll probably pick up at least one additional bet.

But what if someone is sitting out there with a K-Q? In that case a 5 is your only true out, since a 10 would yield a bigger straight to that foe. If you only have four outs, then you're not getting sufficient value for your bet, and you should fold. But, should you fear a K-Q in this situation? Can you put either the bettor or one of the callers on such a naked overcard play? You can if you've been paying attention—you can if you know your foes.

The point of this analysis is to remind us that it's never enough just to do the math. Sure, we need to be able to calculate pot odds and card odds on the fly, but that's where our analysis of the situation begins, not ends.

See the numbers, but
see beyond them, too.

Heaven, Hell, or Limbo?

In a $30–$60 game, you're heads up against a single opponent who called your raise from the small blind. The flop—A♣-9♥-3♦—was favorable to your hand of A♠-J♥. When the small blind checked, you bet and she called. Now the turn comes T♦. The small blind checks. You bet—and she raises. Where are you now and what should you do next?

COMMENT: There comes a time when your thinking about hold'em situations should go beyond the bare decision-making of call/fold/raise and into a more fluid, full-bodied analysis of the circumstances as they unfold. First, ask yourself what your foe might have defended a small blind with. Small pairs and big cards seem likely candidates. If she had a big pair or even A-K, you might have heard about it before or on the flop. Your opponent didn't like the flop enough to bet it, but she did like it enough to call. What could she have? If she's got, say, Q♦-J♦, then the T♦ is a *doubledraw* card for her, a single card yielding both an open-ended straight draw and a flush draw. In most cases (and this is the crucial part of your analysis) your opponent's raise is likely to be a mistake. If she's raising on a draw, or even two draws, she's taking the worst of it in terms of ROI.

If she has put you on a bluff, she's wrong. If she thinks a pair of tens is good, she's wrong. Your opponent is building a pot for you. How nice of her.

Feel free to call.

Sadly, there's another way of looking at this. She started with 9-9 or 3-3 or even A-9, hit the flop hard, and check-called to set up a check-raise on the turn. Can you get away from your hand? Your opponent doesn't think so. That's why she bet. She knows you'll pay off her raise here, and make a crying call on the river.

You should probably fold.

Then again, perhaps your opponent has nothing at all. Maybe she sees that turn card as a juicy opportunity to represent A-T or a set of tens or some other phantom power-house. What a bluffing maniac! Show her who's boss!

Reraise! Definitely reraise!

Okay, so now we have three completely different analyses and three completely different conclusions. Which one is correct? Answer: *There's no way to know!* In this example, you simply don't have enough information about your opponent to know whether she's capable of a big mistake, a straightforward trap play, or a check-raise bluff. What should you do?

Go back in time.

Go back to the moment when this particular foe sat down at your table and *study her.* Note the frequency with which she defends her blinds, and what kinds of cards she has when she does so. Notice whether she *ever* bluffs. (Many players don't, or anyway, don't make these deep, card-dependent bluffs.) Classify her as straightforward or tricky, timid or bold, so that when it comes time to put her on a hand you can do better than guess. Remember, no hand takes place in a vacuum. Bother to learn your foes, or don't bother playing at all.

Planet Steal

Same $30–$60 game, only this time you're in the small blind and this time you *know your foe*. He's a modified blind weevil, someone who will certainly attack blinds from late position, but someone (you've noticed) who will only make this play with any two wheelhouse cards or better. Armed with this knowledge, you have called from the small blind with . . . well, hell, it doesn't even matter what you called with, for you're going to play this hand without cards. The flop came 7-8-2 rainbow, and you check-called to set up a play on the turn. What do you have in mind, and what kind of turn card are you looking for?

COMMENT: Information is power. Knowing your opponent to be a blind-weevil-with-starting-requirements, the only hands you genuinely feared with this flop were the five big pairs, and he was much less likely to have one of those holdings than the aforementioned unpaired wheelhouse cards. Your check-call on the flop looked like a weak, loose call, but it was actually a practical call, looking for a favorable turn card—not a card that hit your hand, but one that fit the play you planned to make. You could afford to make the call because you knew exactly where you're at in this hand: A scare card, such as A, K, or Q will let you slip away from the hand without further damage, but anything from 9 down, roughly two-thirds of the deck, sets up your check-raise gambit. You check, he bets, you raise, he folds. Alternatively, he checks behind your check, effectively surrendering the orphan pot to your river bet.

Two things are required in order to make this play work. The first is *analysis*. You must have a firm fix on your opponent. You must know that he's capable of blind stealing. You must know that he's capable of taking a shot at the pot on the flop with nothing. You must know that he'll take your check-raise as a successful trap play and be able to get away from his hand. In other words, in order to play your opponent effectively on the turn, you must know where he's at before and after the flop. If you've been paying attention (not just in this hand but all along) you'll have all the data you need right here.

The other thing you need is *stones*. You must be prepared to launch and run this program based solely on what you think (*know!*) your opponent has, and on the texture of a favorable flop. It does no good to set up check-raise bluffs such as this if you're not willing to follow them through. *Be* willing. Not only will moves like this put extra chips in your stack, they'll breed fear in your foes, put them off balance, and set up further sophisticated plays downstream. Remember that while it's nice to win a pot, your ultimate goal is *control*.

> If you always need cards to win,
> you're not making the most of
> your game.

Dead (Third) Man Walking

Two wheelhouse players have called your early position preflop raise and you've all seen a flop of Q-T-9 rainbow. Holding A-K, you led at the pot and they both called. Your hand feels fragile, because you've only got overcards and an inside straight draw, and feel it's likely that they hold A-T, A-9, or some kind of jack. You don't put either of them on K-J, for you feel they'd have raised on the flop. Nevertheless, the turn card, an 8, gives you pause. How should you proceed?

A) Bet, and plan to fold if either of them raises.
B) Bet, and plan to call if one raises and the other folds.
C) Check-call no matter what.
D) Check, and plan to fold if either of them bets.
E) Check, and plan to call if one bets and the other folds.

COMMENT: Check, and fold if there's heat. If you were heads up, you might be able to contend, figuring that your outs would at least leave you live on the river. But with two of them in there . . . no. Get out now. Credit them with the hands they have.

You can get yourself into trouble with all sorts of self-justified thinking here. Suppose, for example, that you and the next player both check, and the third player bets. You might hunker down and read the situation from the bettor's point of view: He saw you both check and might therefore reason that the pot is his for the stealing. This may be true, but then again maybe not. Once again we see the importance of having good solid book on your opponents. Is the second player capable of a check-raise here? Is the third player capable of bluffing? If you don't know your foes, you can't make adequate judgments.

But you can do this: Treat all players as straightforward until proven tricky. Only you know the quality of the game you're in, but it's certainly true that there are many more average players out there than superior ones—that's what makes them average. Don't give them credit for more chicanery than they're capable of, not so much because they're not that tricky (they're not) but because we're often a little too tricky for our own good. For the sake of calling, for the sake of not being driven off a pot we somehow feel we deserve (we started with A-K, after all!) we'll rationalize calls on the basis of seeing bluffs that aren't there.

Take your foes at face value until they give you reason to do otherwise. In this way, you can make decisions based on what's real, not on what you wish were real.

DOWN BY THE RIVER

By the time you get to the river, most of your decisions have been made for you. In limit hold'em, the pot is usually so large that it offers odds for many seemingly improbable calls. As has often been pointed out, you can't afford to be routinely wrong for one bet when that one bet could deprive you of 20 or more. This often justifies calls on the river even when you're pretty sure you're beaten. Nevertheless, there are some situations where the attention you've paid throughout the hand can save you—or earn you— extra bets on shakedown street.

Naked Came the Ace

A frisky player raised your big blind, and you called with K♠-J♠. The flop came little-little-little, giving you nothing but overcards, hopes, and dreams. You checked the flop, fully prepared to surrender, but your opponent also checked. When the turn came another brick, you paused to evaluate. You thought you might have the best hand at that point, since Mr. Frisky could have attacked preflop with any two wheelhousers, such as Q-T, and lost his stomach for the fight when faced with a low, raggy, made-to-hit-the-blind-type flop. With this in mind, you went ahead and bet the turn, and Frisky just called. Now the river comes an ace. With about four big bets in the pot, you're first to act. What's your pleasure?

COMMENT: Fans of river bluffs point out that if the pot

is big enough, you don't have to bluff successfully that often in order to turn a profit. If, for example, you're betting $10 into a $90 pot, you can get called almost nine times out of ten and still be in the black on that move. But we're not looking at a big pot here. We're looking at a forlorn, little, scrawny pot just begging for someone to adopt it. Your bet here will certainly make you look like just such a big brother, and may open the door to the one circumstance you don't want to see: a raise back at you. At that point you'll have to ask yourself whether your foe is bluffing, had some of the flop all along, or just now hit his naked ace. Generally speaking, you don't want to make river bets where the only hand that can call you can beat you. If he doesn't have an ace, your hand is probably good—but he also probably won't call. If he does have an ace, you're going to hear about it now. Check. If he checks behind you, you can show down winners. If he bets, you'll have to decide if he's the one who's playing big brother, and proceed accordingly.

> In general, avoid river bets where the only hand that can call you can beat you.

Have a Heart, or Four

You have a *true value* table image, one where people generally believe you to have the hand you represent. Having limped from late position with K♦-Q♠, you saw a flop of J♥-T♥-6♥. It was checked around to you, and you graciously accepted a free card. The turn was a bricky 4♣. A straightforward but aggressive player in early position made a bet and it was folded around to you. Forgetting about pot odds versus card odds, you called the bet and saw the river card heads up. What are you hoping for on the river, and what do you intend to do with it if you get it?

COMMENT: Knowing your foe to be aggressive but straightforward, you viewed his turn bet as an attempt to claim an orphan pot. Perhaps he had a bad jack or a good ten, neither of which he felt confident betting from early position on the flop, but either of which looked worth a shot once the flop got checked around. You recognize that he might have flopped a flush, but we've already discussed what a long-odds proposition that is. The bad jack or good ten are much likelier holdings here. Your call on the turn told him that you hadn't lost interest in the pot, that you're still involved, still looking for something. Now what?

In the best case, you get an ace or a nine to give you a straight. But by calling on the turn, you're actually giving yourself an additional eight river outs, for you plan to bet any fourth heart if your opponent checks to you. Sure, a fourth heart would look scary to you, for your opponent could easily have a heart in his hand. It's probably not a very good one, though, or, he'd have semi-bluffed on the flop. Remember that you have a true value image. When a heart comes on the river, it seems, in your opponent's mind, to complete the exact hand he probably put you on. In this instance, you're not so much bluffing as confirming, by your bet, that you have your opponent beaten. If he's confident in his read, he'll lay down his hand when you bet.

This sort of play doesn't always work, of course. It requires a confluence of circumstances, including a foe who plays a certain way, who views you a certain way and who doesn't have a heart good enough to call with. But just because it doesn't always work doesn't mean you should never make the play. If you only bet when you have the goods, then you are a true value player for real, and you can't hope to take your game to the next level. Here again we see that by planning what to do if certain cards fall, you can use your foe's evaluation of your play to win pots you otherwise can't win.

Something for Nothing

You're in a hand against two other players, one of whom went all-in with his bet on the turn. In there with a *dry draw*—a straight or a flush draw that didn't get there—you're first to act on the river. You figure that the all-in player has a decent holding, but you have no idea where the third player's at. What should you do?

COMMENT: Please check. If you bet and you're called, you lose. If you bet and you're not called, you win exactly zero dollars, the sum total of the empty side pot. You might take some bully-boy satisfaction in having bet the third player off his hand, but to what end? You have squandered a precious bluff opportunity and revealed yourself as a player who makes moves that have no upside.

By the same logic, if you check and your opponent bets, you must fold, for the only hand you can beat is a worse dry draw than yours, and the reward for being right (assuming the all-in player has a real hand) is exactly one bet. Fold. Let the other player have the satisfaction of winning nothing.

The only time you'd want to bet into a dry side pot such as this is if you feel like you've got the all-in player beaten, while the other remaining player has a hand that's better than yours. If you can get him to lay down his winning hand (top pair, weak kicker, for instance, against your second pair, good kicker), thus making your second-best hand good, then go ahead and bet. This actually has a chance of working, *if* your opponent understands the pointlessness of bluffing into a dry side pot. He knows that a bluff has no upside in this situation, so he must conclude that you're not bluffing. Interesting, isn't it? In this situation, you're counting on your foe to be smart enough to realize that you couldn't bet with nothing here, but yet not smart enough to realize that, hey, maybe you could.

Rocky Raccoon Catches Lucky

You have limped late with A-J offsuit, only to have a predictable rocklike player raise his own big blind. The board cards fell your way—A-x-x-x—and you bet and got called by Rocky Raccoon on both the flop and the turn. Now a king hits on the river and Rocky bets out. What thoughts cross your mind while you decide what to do?

COMMENT: Thinking back to the start of the hand, you recall that your opponent raised his own big blind preflop. Most rockish players won't do this without a quality hand, and you're fairly sure that the Rocky Raccoon described here wouldn't have raised without pocket aces, kings, or queens. Since the ace on the flop slowed him down but the king on the river prompted him to bet, you have to figure you're dead to his pocket kings. Fold; fold and don't worry, for Rocky's predictability means it's only a matter of time until he gives the money back.

There's a larger issue here. Success in this situation assumes that you can do two things: put a read on your opponent, and trust the read you have. Many is the hold'em player who has a dead-certain tell on his foe, and yet fails to act according to that tell. In the hand we're looking at here, you knew that your ace was good right up until the river. You maybe even felt smug that your foe couldn't get away from his big pair in the face of that stealth ace. You can sympathize with that predicament, because, hey, we've all been there. But look, when the king comes on the river, suddenly now you *are* there. If you can't get away from your hand when every fiber of your being shouts that you're beaten, then you're ignoring and betraying the very information that makes you a winning player in the first place. Our motto, then:

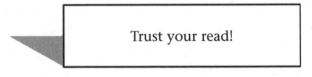

Trust your read!

After all, what's the point of making a read in the first place if you're just going to turn around and pretend it doesn't exist? This is why I asked you what thoughts cross your mind when your opponent bets out. An honest player will admit to feeling at least a little resentment that the hand in which he had the lead now looks to be falling by the wayside. But honesty alone is not enough. *If you knew you were beaten, why in heaven's name did you call?*

In this section we have looked at certain hold'em situations and tried to glean both appropriate strategies and clear lines of thought for dealing with those situations. The fact is that many—dare I say most?—hold'em players do not routinely bring clear lines of thought to the game. They bring strategy, tactics, and perceptions that are wildly torqued by their emotions, expectations, hopes, dreams, and fears. Clear thinking, then, is the necessary first condition for useful analysis. In the next section we're going to look at the world of hold'em through the eyes of some players who lack this essential first condition. It's an enlightening, and in some respects a rather disturbing, view.

3

♣ ♠ ♦ ♥

HOLD'EM DIARIES

♧ ♤ ♢ ♡

A staggering revelation of hold'em comes to us when we start to see the game through the other fellow's eyes. The first time you realize that your foe is as afraid of your bet as you are of his—and you exploit the bluffing opportunity that this breakthrough in thinking affords—you undergo a paradigm shift of no small proportion.

During the play of hands, this business of seeing the action as the other guy sees it is called *ghosting*, and, as I discussed in *Killer Poker: Strategy and Tactics for Winning Poker Play*, it's a useful way to occupy the mind when you've folded a hand and you're keen to keep focused on the game. In this section I'm going to broaden the concept of ghosting by crawling inside the minds of certain types of players and having a thorough look around. And no, I won't be using telepathy. I'm not reading anybody's thought waves like a *Star Trek* alien. All I'm really doing is filtering a basic understanding of the game of hold'em through various players' perspectives.

There's no real trick to this. You use the skill already, and you use it all the time. When you see someone get angry after a bad beat, for example, you have momentary

access to his *literal inner language*. You can almost see it like
a thought balloon over his head.

How do you know this is what he's thinking? Because
it's what you'd be thinking if you were him and if you had
not trained yourself off such irrelevant and unproductive
noise.

One thing I can do that maybe you can't is take these
intuitively understood thoughts and translate them into
words on the page. Well, that's what a writer does: He takes
what everybody else is thinking and puts it out there where
everyone can see it. But I put it to you that if you want to
understand another player, *really* understand him, you could
do worse than to write a few paragraphs describing a poker
situation as you think that player sees it. You do not—I
want to stress this—you do *not* have to be a "writer" in any
sense of the word to profit from this exercise. No one will
see the fruits of your labor except you, and even if you
write something you consider to be, well, really smelly, the
act of having tried will (must!) give you better access to the
thoughts, feelings, and emotions of the player you've at-
tempted to ghost on the page. If you try it even once, you'll
see exactly what I mean. If you do it twice, you'll so immediately get the hang of it that it won't even feel like writing
at all. Do it three times and it's a skill you'll have for life.

Okay, let's get inside some of these characters' heads.
Following each "diary," we'll have some commentary and
deconstruction.

Lucy Loosely

They call the game "Texas hold'em," you know, not "Texas throw 'em away." I mean, jeepers, if I didn't want to gamble, I'd have stayed home watching poker on TV. That's why I play poker, and in fact that's why I play hold'em. Omaha's too slow for me. They spend all that time figuring out who had what and then splitting the pot . . . b-o-o-r-i-n-g! Give me hold'em any day: flop, turn, river, showdown . . . next case! I want action!

And in fact, I want action on every single hand. Any time I pick up two cards, I wanna see something playable. Yes, I deserve to see something playable because I didn't drive all the way from Pacoima to fold. If I were honest with myself (which, okay, I'm not, not really) I would realize that this feeling is so strong that it actually turns unplayable cards into playable ones in my mind.

Here's how that works.

I'm in late position. I've been exercising real discipline, throwing away hands like J-3 offsuit and 6-2 suited (almost playable!) and it's been, like, wow, almost a whole entire lap since I've had something worthwhile even by my dizzy standards. Now here come my cards. Like I usually do, I look at them one at a time, which gives me a little extra buzz, a tiny extra bit of thrill, because, like, if that first card is an ace then I can start to root for the second card to be an ace, too. Pocket aces, woo-hoo! How come I can't get them every hand?

Yes, I know the odds against picking up pocket aces are umpty-zumpty-something to one. I'm not completely ignorant, you know. I just want what I want, that's all. Is that so bad? Everyone wants what they want. Right now I want good cards.

But the first card is a 7, and that's not a promising start. At this point I'm hoping for a second 7 or at least a suited ace (or, okay, suited king), but the second card isn't any of those, it's a 6, a sucky 6, sucky offsuit too, to boot. Okay, I'm not suited but I'm connected and I'm in late position, so if there's enough callers in front of me I can profitably limp in and hope to hit a straight. I read that in a book somewhere. I don't remember the exact language of it, but it was written by one of those authors, so it has to be true, and what they said was even any hand is playable if you're getting the right odds. I think that's what it was. Anyway, I'm thinking to myself that I'm only gonna play the hand if there are three or four people in the pot before me and it's not raised, but by the time it gets to me only one person has called. But he's the sort of uptight prig who only plays high cards, so I figure if I hit my 7 or my 6 my hand will be good, so I call. But then the doofus in the small blind raises and of course I have to call that raise because I didn't drive all the way from Pacoima to fold, especially not after I've already put in one bet, and that's called protecting your investment, right?

Three of us see the flop, and it comes 6-T-T and I'm happy because there's only two other 10s in the deck, and how likely is it that only one of two opponents has only one of two cards? When the small blind bets I assume he's just trying to steal the pot, which is his big fat mistake because I have two pair, and I just know that's the best hand now. The other player calls but I don't pay much attention to that. Since he's the sort of player who only plays with high cards (I think), he probably has only high cards and he will be sad when my 6s hold up. I just call because I don't want to give away the strength of my hand, but there's a raise on the turn with my name on it, you betcha.

The turn card is an ace. That slows down the small blind. He just checks and we all know he's beaten. But then the other player bets and oops, he's a player who likes high cards, so maybe he likes that ace a lot.

Or maybe not, you know? When you think about it, there are other high cards beside an ace. There's kings, queens, and jacks too, and probably that's what he's got, like K-J or Q-J. He knows the small blind is afraid of the ace, so he's betting here to steal the pot. I suppose he expects me to fold.

But I didn't drive all the way from Pacoima to fold!

I should probably raise, just to put the fear on him, but then I'd lose the small blind who, after all, might just contribute another bet to my pot if I let him. So I just call and the small blind calls, and we see the river, and it's a 6 and who's got the best hand now?!

A bunch of bets later I find out that it's, crap, not me. The small blind has A-6. (And he raised preflop with that? What kind of hoonyack is he?) The other player, wouldn't you know it, had J-T suited and he was dumb-lucky enough to flop three of a kind and win the pot with 10s full.

Shrug it off, Lucy. Here come your next cards. The first one is a jack. Hold your breath . . . the next one might be a jack as well!

COMMENT: I love Lucy. I do. I have tremendous sympathy for her. I know what it's like to crave action. I know what it's like to *fold, fold, fold* when you just want to *play, play, play.* I like to think that I'm smart enough and self-aware enough not to fall into the action-trap that Lucy falls into. But I also know that sometimes I slip. Sometimes I get so impatient for premium cards that junk starts to look playable to me. It's the textbook definition of *subjective reality,* of course: *The hand you folded an hour ago is the hand you raise with now.* Can you honestly claim that you've never experienced a similar urge? Or is it fair to say that, at the end of the day, there's a little Lucy in all of us?

Lucy's thinking is flawed; of course it's flawed. But you know what? Flawed thinking happens all the time. If it's true that there are higher levels of thinking than yours, it's also true that there are lower levels of thinking than yours. Part of successful ghosting is knowing what type of errors your opponents make, and why. The small blind's preflop raise with A-6, for instance, was not as wrong as Lucy imagines, not if he knows her well. He figures she'll call with worse hands, so he can go ahead and raise, and take his chances with the other limper.

Lucy's mistakes all have the same root cause: her need for action. Knowing this, you now know not just that she makes mistakes, but the whole, specific *class* of mistakes she tends to make.

With that in mind, let's do an exercise in prognostication. Aside from just generally playing too loose, what sort of specific errors would you expect a Lucy Loosely to make? I'll start you off.

1. She'll defend all blinds.
2. She'll play tired.
3. She'll start playing the moment she sits down, with-

out waiting for position and without taking the time to get to know her foes.

Now you.

4. _____
5. _____
6. _____

Now knowing what you know about Lucy, can you devise some specific strategies to use against her? Here are some things I'd do.

If I'm sitting on her right, I'll tend to call, rather than raise, in order to open the door to her involvement. If I'm sitting on her left, I'll raise to isolate. I won't be worried that she'll suddenly wise up and fold; that's just not in her nature. I'll bet most flops that I have a piece of. Her loose calls took her this far, and they'll take her further still. A genuine Lucy Loosely will call even with nothing, hoping it will turn into something sometime. I'll bet for value on the end, for Lucy is more likely than the average player to call with a losing hand. She said herself that she didn't come all the way from Pacoima to fold—even when she knows she's beat.

And you? How would you beat Lucy?

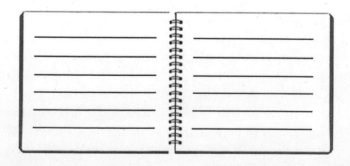

We can expect to take some bad beats at the hands of a player like Lucy. Since she'll call with anything, she'll turn over some surprising winning hands from time to time. As Killer Poker players, we have learned to take these beats in stride. It's okay if she wins once in a while. Her thinking is so unsound that she'll give it all back in the end—unless we chase her away by being rude or angry at her when she sucks out.

Hold'em, as we know, is a game of decisions. With Lucy, as with any player whose decision-making process is fundamentally flawed, we want to put her to as many decisions as possible. Every time she chooses wrong we're making money, so pressure is the name of our game. We may not bust her on this hand, but we'll definitely bust her in the end.

Big Richard

It's about me. Of course it's about me. Baby, it's all about me. When I sit down at the poker table, you chumps are going to know I'm there! With my table talk and my body language and, most of all, my bets, I will make my presence known. Why? Because Big Richard is a bully, and how else does a bully behave? For the sake of feeling superior, I will push people around. It's what gets me off. It's why I play poker in the first place. I don't just want your money, I want to see that look on your face.

I want to see you sweat.

When I'm in the pot, I'm in the pot. If I think there's a chance I can steal, I'll steal. If I'm good for a call, I'm good for a raise. I have two speeds: fast and supersonic. If you get into a betting war with me, I won't be the one who blinks. Play with me for any length of time and you will fear me.

You might not respect me. You might even think I'm wrong to play the way I do, but I don't care. You exist only to serve my need: to feel good about me.

I want to _own_ the game when I play, and the way I do that is by being the dominant force, the bully, the slavemaster, the one that everyone defers to, the one who makes them tremble. Or put it another way: Only the bus driver knows which way the bus is going. So I'm gonna drive the bus. I'm gonna define the style and the tempo of the game. I'm gonna raise a lot and check-raise a lot. And if you try to bully me back, I will bully you back. I own the final raise.

I understand that being the boss is a pretty effective strategy for winning poker, but that's not why I play this way. Nope, it's ego. Pure and simple, ego. I need the world to acknowledge my greatness and superiority, and if the poker table is the only place I can get that need met, then that's where you'll find me, getting it met.

Out there in the real world, I work in what they call the "service sector." I wear a shirt with my name stitched over the pocket, and I have to be polite to yammerheads all day long. It's no wonder that by the end of the day when I finally get to play poker I'm fairly climbing the walls with frustration and rage. I come straight from work to play poker. (You know I do, 'cause I'm still wearing my shirt with the name stitched over the pocket.) And once I get to the table, I'm going to take it out on anyone who gets in my way. I've got some steam to blow off, and someone's gonna get scalded. Count on it.

Naturally with an approach like mine you get

into a lot of pissing contests with other players. I
don't care. I live for that. Say I'm holding K-Q
and the flop comes A-K-x. I'll open. Of course I'll
open. I'm not the kind of neeny to leave a flop like
that unbet. You wanna raise? Go right ahead. I'll
raise you back so fast it'll make your head spin.
You'd think I'd put you on an ace or even A-K, but
I won't. I'm much more likely to think you're
screwing with me than to think you have a real
hand. Why? Because if I were you, I'd be screwing
with me, and that's the way I see the game.
Playing as I do inside a macho fog, I assume that
everyone else plays in the same macho fog. (Except
you ladies—hey, can I buy you a drink?) So go
ahead and bet into me if you like. But you'd better
know that I won't back down, no matter how
much it costs.

Here's the kind of confrontation I love.

I'm in the big blind and you bring it in for a
raise. Of course I raise back, because I absolutely
will not have you thinking you can bully my
blinds. I might have a hand in this situation, but
then again I might not. Mostly what I have is this
sense of entitlement that says I get to raise your
blinds but you don't get to raise mine.

Anyway, you raise my blind, so I raise you back
and you just call, weak neeny that you are. Now
here's what I know that you don't know: I'm
gonna bet any flop. If you call, I'm gonna bet the
turn. If you call, I'm gonna bet the river. I don't
care what cards you have. I don't care what cards
I have. I'm gonna keep pounding you with bets
until you cry uncle and throw your hand in.

And when you do, I'm gonna laugh. I'm gonna

laugh my ass off, because I won the pot, but I won something even better: <u>dominance</u>. I own this table, and there's not a damn thing you can do about it. If I really want to rub salt in your sad wounds, I'll show you the cheese I beat you with. Why? 'cause I want you to <u>suffer</u>. I want you to feel <u>bad</u>. And again, I understand that there's good solid strategy reasons for making you suffer like that, but again that's not why I do it. I just want to <u>inflict</u>. That's the kind of guy I am.

So bring it with you when you come, but you'd better bring all of it, because I never back down. I am the biggest Richard at this table, though many people call me Dick.

COMMENT: Big Richard is doing a lot of things right. His aggressiveness, his fearlessness, his bully behavior— these are all tools that a Killer Poker player knows and values and employs. But Big Richard isn't playing Killer Poker, not by a long shot, because he's doing all these right things for all these wrong reasons. He said it himself, he's not interested in the money. He just wants to inflict.

You see his type all the time: people who bring to the table their feelings of anger and frustration and rage, and stack them there like so many stacks of chips. Maybe he's had a bad day at work (with a guy like Richard, they're probably mostly bad days). Maybe he's got troubles at home (with a guy like Richard, also quite likely). For whatever reason, know this: Richard plays the way he plays because he's improperly processing some crap from the outside world. He wants to win—to dominate and crush— for no other reason than to stop feeling bad about himself. The guy could use some therapy, but that's not the point.

A player like Richard can be a formidable foe. His

scorched-earth policy gives him a high degree of control at the table, and his invulnerability to raises and reraises makes it very difficult for anyone else (such as sensible, aggressive players like us) to wrest that control away. Even though we know what Richard is doing, and even though we know why (better even than he knows, maybe), we still end up playing Dick's game. Not good. We Killer Poker players don't want the initiative in anyone's hands but ours.

What to do? How can you use Richard's big stick (or word that rhymes with *stick*) against him?

First, acknowledge that sometimes you can't. Sometimes a guy like Big Richard is such a powerful force at the table that the only thing to do is just *get the hell out of there.* You might not want to do that. You might not want to run away because it will look to Richard like you're running scared. You know what? Let it. So what if he then gets to feel superior? As an emotionally balanced player (unlike Richard), you don't care what other players think.

In certain circumstances you won't want to, or be able to, get out of Richard's way. It may be that the game you're both in is an otherwise excellent game, or it may be that it's the only game going. In that case, you're going to have to make some adjustments. Here are a few I can think of.

- Tighten up against him. Make sure that when you go to war against Richard, you have superior weapons. You don't want to be in a situation where you know he's got nothing, but you still can't go after him because, sadly, you've got nothing either. Richard is bluff-proof. You're going to have to beat him with cards.
- Trap more often. Let him do your betting for you.
- Prepare for high volatility. Richard puts a lot of chips into play, and he requires that those who play against him do the same. Mentally gird yourself for fluctua-

tion. Remember that Richard's principle weapon is fear. If you go in unafraid, you take away much of his strength.

- Be his friend. To some degree you can neutralize or deflect his bully behavior by just being nice. Show interest and empathy. Players such as Richard perceive everyone around them as either an enemy or a victim. If you're neither of these things, he will unconsciously soften up against you, and direct his fury elsewhere.
- Or be his enemy.

Why would being his enemy be an effective strategy against Big Richard?

As we noted with Lucy, if players are prone to a certain class of mistakes, you generally want to coax them further down that wrong road. If you present yourself to Richard as his enemy—his rival for control of the table—well, it's like waving a red flag in front of a bull. His rage will run roughshod over his judgment. He will become convinced that he can dominate on the strength of that rage alone. When the universe presents him with evidence to the contrary, he'll play even more furiously, and even more incorrectly. He will become a tilt-bomb, and his explosion will spew shrapnel, in the form of chips, all over the table.

Scaredy Scarederson

I've been playing hold'em in casinos for about a year now, ever since I read a few books and graduated from my home game. I think I have a pretty good game. I'm tight, anyhow, so that's good. I know how to fold and I know how to wait. But I do seem to lose more than I win, and sometimes I lose by the buttload. I don't know what it is. I hate to say it, but I've come to believe that I'm jinxed somehow. I just don't feel like I can win.

Well, anyway, I don't want to keep losing by the buttload, so to protect myself from that, I don't bring a whole lot of cash to the club. Also, I always buy in for the table minimum, and that way I don't risk more than I have to.

Strangely, that doesn't seem to work too well.

Take last night when I went down to the Progress Casino, my local club here in beautiful and scenic Progress, California. Even before I got off the freeway and parked my car, I felt all edgy and jumpy and jangly, like I'd had too much coffee to drink. And you know what? This happens every time. The very sight of that big neon sign (PROGRESS CASINO —WHERE WINNERS ARE NOT RESENTED!) sets my heart racing and my palms sweating. I don't know why that is.

Anyway, I found a seat in a $3-$6 hold'em game and I bought in for $30. I waited for the blinds to pass and posted behind the button. That's conservative, smart play, right? Well, some joker in early position raised me on my very first hand. I had pretty good cards, A-9, but I was determined to play tight, so I folded. Wouldn't you know it? Mr. Jokerman had nothing. He even showed me

the 7-T crudola he raised with, which I think he
did just to vex me.

But I was cool. I was. It'll take more than just
some betting fool to put me off my game. I kept on
playing tight—which was easy considering the junky
hands I kept picking up. Three laps later, I was down
to less than half my buy-in. That's when I took a
shot with J-Q suited and saw the flop heads-up with
the very same joker as before. The flop came K-6-3,
and Mr. Jokerman bet out. I knew he wanted me to
think he had a king, but I remembered his earlier
crudola from before and I wasn't fooled. Even
though I only had overcards... or no, not overcards, more like undercards, I guess... anyways, I
called him. When a queen came on the turn I
called all-in, but damn if he didn't have K-T and
damn if he didn't win the pot. See what I mean by
jinxed? Some people are just not lucky.

Well, the night kind of went downhill from
there. I put the same short buy-in on the table
three or four more times, until my pockets were
empty. That's when I thought about the ATM in the
lobby and thought, What the hell, right? My luck's
bound to turn around sometime. But it never did.
I just couldn't get anything started. And people
kept playing very aggressively against me. Like
they didn't even want to let me into the pot. Not
just Jokerman, all of them. And then when I did
get in, I couldn't get any action. Like this one
time when I picked up pocket aces and raised before the flop? Everyone folded. I must be too easy to
read. But why should that matter if I'm only playing premium cards?

I guess I don't get this game.

I feel a little sick to my stomach.

COMMENT: Whenever you encounter short money, consider it scared money and attack it exactly like a lion peels the weak or sick springboks from the herd. Why should you consider short money to be scared money? Hey, if it's not scared money, what kind is it? Ignorant? That's possible. It's possible that your opponent doesn't know better than to buy in short, but okay, ignorant money plays as weakly as scared money. It's remotely possible, I suppose, that the short buy-in is coming from an otherwise superior player who's temporarily strapped for funds—though if he's really that superior, why is he strapped? For that matter, if he really is superior, why doesn't he drop down to a limit where his bankroll is adequate for the game? Expert players don't go to war in fixed-limit hold'em games without sufficient weaponry; therefore, those who do are, prima facie, not expert.

It's also within the realm of possibility that an expert player is masquerading as a Scaredy Scarederson, immersing himself in the role even to the extent of handicapping himself with the short buy-in. If you run into an expert foe so deeply deceptive that he can actually pull off the innocent act, more power to him; he probably has other weapons with which to beat you down as well.

Scaredy Scarederson, though, is no expert, and his short buy-in is only the first sign of this. His betting patterns also reveal his fear. Any time you see a player who's prone to check-calling and check-folding, and unwilling to raise all but his strongest hands, you're looking at someone more concerned with *not losing* than with *winning*. And no, this is not your garden variety rock. A rock plays *tight*. A frightened player plays *weak*. The distinction lies not in starting requirements but in betting actions after the start. A rock plays his infrequent starts actively. A Scaredy Scarederson plays his infrequent starts passively. Know a frightened player by the infrequency of his raises.

As if that weren't enough, Scaredy's very own body betrays his fear. Scaredy himself points out that he arrives at the club all flushed and shaky and nervous. Why? Adrenaline: his body's own response to fight-or-flight situations. He is an inexperienced poker player, for whom the very act of *going to play poker* still generates a buzz. He likes that buzz—it's why he enjoys playing poker. But he doesn't have enough experience with it (hasn't become sufficiently inured to it) to keep it from taking over his physical being. Because he's putting money at risk, and because he unconsciously equates money with survival, he's getting an inevitable and inexorable body response.

Look for the predictable signs. Take note of shaking hands and furtive glances and even beads of sweat. And when you spot them, go after them, for here we have another player whose decisions are bent by forces he can't control. His fear of losing will cause him to err on the side of caution. Force him to make many decisions and you widen this hole in his play like greenhouse gasses open ozone holes.

It's easy to feel fear when you don't know what you're doing, and the fact is that Scaredy doesn't know what he's doing. He hasn't played enough or studied enough to see how easily his foes can victimize him. He's in a tough position—one that every beginning player has been in. He needs to gain experience in order to gain confidence, but until he acquires that experience, his lack of confidence will betray him and cost him money. You could say that this is the price of his poker education, and to his credit he's paying for it at a suitably low limit.

Then again, you don't find frightened players only at entry-level limits. Any time a player plays higher than he's used to, he's at risk for letting the weight of money push him off proper play. Once more we see the sheer damn utility of knowing your opponents. If you know a certain foe to frequent limits like $10–$20 and below, and now suddenly one day you find him taking a shot at $30–$60, consider him scared until proven brave. If he's underfunded, or absent courage, he's making a strategic mistake that may lead to all sorts of tactical ones as well. Amplify his mistakes by putting him to as many decisions as possible.

Also be aware that, sad to say, there's a little Scaredy Scarederson in all of us. At one time or another we all play nervous. Maybe we're stepping up in limits, or maybe we're up against a tough field, or famous players. It's no sin to be scared, but it is a sin to let fear adversely affect our play. So I would ask you now to identify the threads of fear that color the coat of your hold'em play.

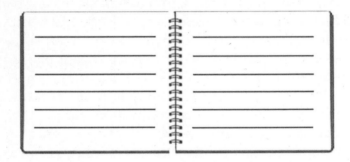

Mad Cow

"Maniac!" That's how those bozos view me when they see me in there raising from early position with 4-5 offsuit. They call me Mad Cow, and they think I'm a <u>terrible, dreadful, awful</u> player. They laugh up their sleeves at me. They talk behind their hands about me. They call me names. They hate and loathe and mock me, and you know what? I don't give a rat's ass! Why? Because I <u>am</u> a maniac, and maniacs just don't care!

Lemme tell you, there's lots of counterfeit mani-

acs out there. They dress up their play in a cloak of outrageous image. I don't respect those guys. They lack the courage of their convictions. A true maniac will raise with <u>anything! Anytime!</u> A true maniac doesn't bother to calculate odds. A true maniac takes slim draws without blinking. A true maniac four-bets it preflop with T-2. A true maniac's stack goes up and down like a yo-yo. And in his mind the true maniac is thinking, That's the way, uh-huh, uh-huh, I like it, uh-huh, uh-huh.

Take it from me, if you're up against Mad Cow, you might as well be playing against a space alien. You think you're playing hold'em, but that's not the game Mad Cow is playing. No, Mad Cow is playing a different game where nothing matters but throwing bets into the pot and seeing what happens next. Hold'em is a coin flip game to me, and I don't care about anything so much as <u>getting that next coin in the air.</u>

Any two will do. That's my motto and my mantra. Tell me you've never flopped a full house with 5-2 offsuit. I've done it more than once, and the rush I got from flopping that beauty makes me want to do it again and again and again. How the hell can I hit my flop if I fold my hand? Can't. Can't-can't-can't. So don't expect me to fold, 'cause I don't.

And don't expect me to just call, either, 'cause I don't. Calling is for wimps, for people who don't like action. I like action. I like it twice as much as you do, so I put in twice as many bets as you do. It's funny to me how upset this gets you. Really. You should see your red face and your pouty little look.

I've taken your quiet, safe $20-$40 game and turned it into a balls-out mandatory $40-$80. Why? Because I can, that's why. And because (do I have to spell it out for you?) it gives me more a-c-t-i-o-n.

Now you look around the table and you see that Mad Cow's disease is starting to affect the other players. Suddenly they're calling raises with T-9 suited, little pairs, all kinds of kibbles and bits that they'd throw away without a second thought if old Mad Cow weren't in the game. They're drooling to get my money, poor saps, and it's taking them right out of their game.

You won't be sucked in like that, will you? No, you're going to tighten up your starting requirements even more, so that when you're in a hand against ol' Cow, you'll <u>know</u> you have the best of it. That's a fool's paradigm, Alice. It won't do you any good. You'll be outvoted by the rest of the table: The raises and reraises will be coming so fast and furious, you won't be able to get a bet in edgewise. So then you'll start to whisper seductive reasoning into your own ear. "I'll just limp in," you'll say. "I could hit a flop, and when I do, I'll win a monster pot." Before you know it, you're on the raisin' train with everyone else. Mad Cow is the conductor, and there's a bridge out ahead!

You just don't get it, do you? I don't want your money. I don't care about money. I love the attention. I love being the lightning rod for the game. Or I may be drunk, for ol' Bessie can put away the bevvies. It doesn't matter what my motivation is. All that matters is the effect I have on the game.

I'm the only one playing by my rules, and your efforts to adjust are futile—futile, I say!—because your strategies may change, but your goal remains the same. You want to win.

I just wanna rock!

It drives you nutso, doesn't it? Here's a guy, a genuine Mad Cow, who seems like a lock to give all his money away. You can't loosen up too much, because if you do you won't have any card edge over me. But if you don't loosen up at all, you're letting everyone else at the table get my money instead of you. But you know that they're loosening up—they have to be in order to compete against <u>la vaca loca</u>—and since they're loosening up, you might as well loosen up, too. Get your fair share. Come on in, you big, soft schmoo, the water's fine!

Why do I play this way? I already told you—action. But if you want a deeper answer, I'll give you a peek at my tattoo. It says BORN TO LOSE. *Ever since I can remember, I was told what a loser I was. Then I discovered poker and I said, "Hey, here's a place where I don't have to be a loser." And then sometimes I won, but sometimes I lost, but I discovered that I felt pretty much the same, win or lose. Sure it's nice to win, because then you have all this extra money and money is cool. But losing is cool too, because, hey, I'm born to lose, right? And if I lose, at least I'm fulfilling my destiny. There's something comforting about being the loser everyone always told me I was.*

For years I said the sky was falling and everyone said I was crazy. Then the sky fell. Well, at least I wasn't crazy.

You don't believe me, I know. You just can't

comprehend that there are people out there who not only don't care whether they win or lose, they actually feel better about themselves when they piss their money away. Good for you. I'm happy for you. You can't imagine ever taking satisfaction in walking away from the table saying, "God, what a loser I am." Fine. You have a tiny imagination. How is that my fault?

But before you dismiss me as a figment of someone's imagination, think about cutters, teenagers who slice themselves with knives or razors, or pierce or brand themselves. (True fact; you could look it up.) They're sad kids, these cutters, but I tell you I can see them from where I stand. The wounds they self-inflict are painful, sure, but it sure makes them know they're alive. To quote my man Warren Zevon, "I'd rather feel bad than feel nothing at all."

And don't forget that when I feel good, I feel way better than you. My style of play leads to some stunning losses—but also to some breathtaking wins. And when I walk away from the table with rack upon rack upon rack of chips (your chips, my chimp) I get the satisfaction not just of beating you, but of beating you <u>on my terms.</u> Who's the mad cow now?

Sure, sure, sure, I'll probably come back tomorrow and pee all my profit back into the game. But that's tomorrow. For now I leave you devastated by a style of play you can't comprehend, can't emulate, can't counter. So you vow that next time we meet you won't buy into The Madness of King Cow. You tell yourself you'll stay sane, be patient, play tight, and trust that I can't buck the odds

forever. Know what? Maybe you're right. Maybe I can't buck the odds forever.
   But I guess I'll die trying.

COMMENT: Some people doubt that the Mad Cow really exists. They consider him, like the Loch Ness Monster or Bigfoot, to be a myth or a legend born out of fear or ignorance. They claim that most alleged maniac sightings are, in fact, incidents of idiots who just don't know what they're doing. True maniacs, genuine kamikaze pilots of the green felt, they claim, are rare as a tightwad's toke.

There's a word for people who doubt the existence of maniacs, and the word is: wrong.

Maniacs do exist. They may not be as psychologically shredded as our friend Mad Cow, but they're out there, and for whatever dark and depraved reason they take our hold'em game, turn it upside down, and shake it till the change falls out.

It's usually a change for the worse.

We think it shouldn't be. We see Mad Cow going off for four bets with a hand like K♠-3♥ and we commence to lick our chops. The problem is not so much the maniac, but all the other chop-lickers sitting out there with us, also drawing a bead. And the problem for all of us is that the maniac is warping reality. We try to continue playing hold'em, but the game has become something altogether else.

Consider: You've got a maniac seated on your right, just where you think you want him. He makes his standard pre-flop raise, and you put him on some random hand all the way down to 7-2 offsuit. In fact, for the sake of this example, let's say that the Mad Cow has accidentally flashed his hand and you *know* he's holding 7-2 offsuit. Of course you raise with your J-T suited; you'd raise with anything here. It so happens that your J-T suited is better than a 2-1 favorite over 7-2, so you're pretty happy with those odds, if only you can isolate Mad Cow and play him heads up. The problem is you can't possibly isolate Mad Cow here, because:

A) The rest of the table knows he's a Mad Cow and they know what you're trying to do.
B) Everyone else's starting requirements have plummeted, just as yours have.

As a consequence, anyone sitting behind you with a naked ace or a pocket pair of any kind will figure themselves to be a favorite over your semi-strong hand and Mad Cow's random noise. They're not, as it happens; when you set J-T suited up against 7-2 offsuit and, say, a pair of eights, J-T is still favored against either hand. Alas, it's not favored against both. Plus, anyone with a decent flush draw or suited connectors will be right in there too, calculating that all the action in front of them now makes their draw a net-plus proposition. Suddenly your 2-1 favorite against 7-2 offsuit becomes a dramatic underdog to a full field. You've done the right thing for the right reason, and gotten an inevitable wrong result, not because Mad Cow is a blunderer—he is—but because everyone else knows it, too. So then we might say

> The trouble with a maniac is you don't get him all to yourself.

Just as a maniac turns a conventional game upside down, playing against a maniac requires that we turn conventional wisdom upside down. Conventional wisdom says to put the maniac on your right where you can raise to isolate. But we've just seen the trap that puts us in. Nor do we want to put the maniac on our left, so he can abuse us with raises every time we try to sneak into a pot. Where, then, to place the cow? It seems to me that the best place to put the maniac is directly across from you—and not just so you can stare into his beady little eyes and try to figure out what drugs he's on.

If there are three or four players between you and the maniac, and then three or four players yet to act after you, you end up enjoying the best of both worlds. You can get a sense of how the players in front of you gauge their hands, while affording yourself some leverage over players yet to act.

Scenario: That same Mad Cow has that same 7-2, but now you're three or four seats downstream. He raises under the gun and the player to his left raises to isolate. It's folded around to you. If you three-bet here, you can drive out all but the strongest hands, because even though they suspect you're not super-strong, it will now cost them three bets— probably four, given the likelihood of a Mad Cow cap—to back their hunch. Limpers can't limp and bullies can't bully. You've taken control of the hand.

And put a legitimate, straightforward player between yourself and the maniac.

Don't sit to the right of the maniac. *Don't* raise to isolate. Let someone else do your dirty work for you. Then if you have junk, you fold, but if you have a hand, you can three-bet it, let the maniac four-bet it, and put the player in the middle to a hard and costly choice. In the best case, he'll lose stomach for the fight and drop out, leaving you heads-up against the maniac—exactly where you wanted to be— with extra dead money in the pot. Delicious! In sum, then,

> Don't raise the maniac.
> Reraise the maniac's raiser.

What we're talking here is hammer-and-anvil, where the maniac is the anvil, you are the hammer, and the player in the middle is the thing that gets beaten. Change your focus from playing against the Mad Cow to playing against the rest of the table. While they're all still busy trying to respond to this flurry of weird, unwarranted betting, you be busy figuring out counter-moves to the moves the other players make.

Should you find yourself sitting to the left of the maniac, you can yet use this strategy to similar effect. Simply call with your premium or semi-premium hands. Players behind you will figure you for a Limpy Limperson (first cousin to a Scardy Scarderson), and assume that their raises will put the squeeze on you and Mad Cow alike. When Mad Cow reraises, *you* claim the last raise for your own. Neither of your opponents will know where you're at. Cow won't know because Cow won't notice. The other player, the straightforward one with at least a semi-strong hand, won't know whether you're slow-play/trapping or reraising as a function of Mad Cow disease. If the flop comes high, he'll worry that you trapped. If the flop comes low, he'll worry that you hit your cheese. In short, he'll be lost on the hand against two opponents who could have anything at all.

And your post-flop strategy? Same as preflop: Let the workers do your work for you. If the maniac bets and you like your hand, you can either raise to isolate, or just call along, to represent a trap or trap for real. If the maniac just checks (unlikely for true Mad Cows) you can either bet to control or check to check-raise. Your strength is two-fold: You have position over the maniac, and rough knowledge of the third player's relative strength.

There's much more I could say about playing against Mad Cows, but I wonder what strategies and tactics you yourself can devise.

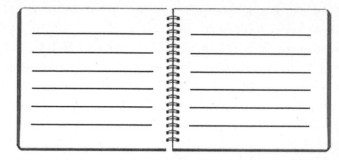

Next time you're in a game against a genuine maniac, remember that *everyone is watching the maniac*. Don't do that. Instead, watch the other players, especially the supposedly strong, knowledgeable ones. Note how they skew their strategies and/or surrender their starting requirements. These are short-sighted, greedy people. They see the maniac's money, and they want to *get some now*. What they don't seem to realize is that there's only one Mad Cow at the table, but six or seven sheep following along. Let them focus on slaughtering the cow. You go shear the sheep.

Fakiac

I am a cork bobbing on the sea of poker. I'm floating on mountainous waves of raises and reraises. I've lost all judgment. I have no common sense. I will bet anywhere, anytime, with anything, for I don't know good cards from bad. I play with my bile, not my brain. I am completely, totally, utterly, desperately out of control. I have no hope. Before the night is done I will lose my money, shirt, dignity, and self-respect. It has to be this way, for no one could play as boldly badly as I play and expect to come out on top. I am a loser with a capital L!

Or so it would seem.

So it would seem to you.

Welcome to the nightmare world of the Fakiac. Look at me and what do you see? Mr. Drunk? Mr. Angry? Mr. Stupid? Mr. High? Mr. Nonsense? Mr. Careless? Mr. Clueless? I could be any one of these people. Or rather, I could seem to be any one of these people. Buy into my image and I will crush you. Not only that, you'll never know what hit you. Not only that, you'll probably come back for more.

I'm not a maniac, but I play one at the poker table. I'm a Fakiac, a fake maniac, and if you don't get wise to the difference, you will be dashed upon the rocks of my superior play. You will think I'm a Mad Cow. You'll play me like a cow and make all the adjustments you should make against a cow. But I'm not a cow. I don't play terrible cards—though I seem to. I don't raise with reckless abandon—though I seem to. I don't steam, I don't tilt, I don't play angry poker or revenge poker or toxic self-destructo poker—though I seem to.

Why do I play the way I play? Simple. I want to win. I want to win all the money I can. I want to win with good cards, bad cards, any cards, and no cards. I have discovered that the Fakiac image is a powerful tool for loosening the screws of an otherwise tight game and making everyone— everyone but me, that is—start to play less and less correctly. I appear to be a suicide bomber, but I'm not. I have a bulletproof vest.

You thought I was a Mad Cow when I three-bet in late position with T-9 offsuit. You thought that was a crazy move, and maybe it was, from your perspective. But you didn't know what I knew: The original raiser plays strictly kosher poker. I could reliably put him on big paint or big pairs. And the blinds, yet to act behind me, were congenital folders who could be counted on to leave me heads-up against one player with a superior hand—but a hand I had fairly well defined.

The flop came 9-6-3. Okay, that's a favorable flop. Sometimes flops are favorable. What're you gonna do? I could've still got drawn out on, but I didn't. That happens. And if I'd gotten drawn out on, so what? I'd have lost a few bets, but I don't care about a few bets. I'm thinking big picture. You're thinking about saving a few bets while I'm thinking about running the table. Whose chances do you like in the long run? I like mine.

And here's a secret: <u>Because</u> I like my chances, and because I like my style, I'm much more likely to play confident poker against you than you are likely to play confident poker against me. That gives me more edge. Plus, I know what I'm doing, but you don't think I do. Like I said, you think I'm a Mad Cow. You saw me push that T-9 or that 8-7 or that little pocket pair and you think I play that way all the time. Now all I have to do is keep chattering away, meanwhile snugging up my starting requirements. I'll be out ahead of you on hand after hand and you won't believe it because you're still seeing me as a maniac. But I'm not. I'm a Fakiac. And that makes all the difference in the world.

COMMENT: The Fakiac has the best of all possible worlds. He distorts reality like a maniac and torques the table like a maniac, but he does so without the maniac's self-destructive flaws of low self-esteem or gambling addiction. If you have the discipline, table sense, acting skills, and fortitude to pull it off, the Fakiac image is definitely one you should go for.

How do you turn yourself into a Fakiac? For starters, pad your bankroll. Whatever you're used to buying in for, buy in for twice that amount, for this is a circumstance where you not only anticipate wild fluctuation, you actually encourage it. Your goal is to destabilize the table, and if you succeed, you will create a highly volatile, *big action* poker game, where everyone is playing outside their comfort zone, but the only one doing so correctly is you.

Next, *talk the talk.* There are a number of ways to do this. You can present yourself as drunk or clueless or insane or tilty or angry at the world. Whatever image you choose, remember that you have taken on an *acting assignment,* and you can't drop the act until your time at the table is done.

Is it possible for someone who is known to others as a strong, straightforward player to sell the Fakiac image? Of course it is. Everyone has bad days, right? Come into the club bitching about the traffic or your bills or the fam damily or even the weather. Growl at the floorman to sell you some extra chips, 'cause you feel like going to *war.* Let your anger or resentment show. Be—well, *seem* to be—completely controlled by your emotions. Play like you *want to feel pain.*

Okay, there you are with a chip on your shoulder and a mound of chips to bet with. You're loaded for bear and everyone knows it. Here's where your fortitude comes in.

In order to make your Fakiac image look like genuine Mad Cow, you're going to have to throw off some bets. Do this early in the session and make sure the fact is known. The ideal circumstance would be to raise under the gun with something like 7-6 suited and—*mirabile visu*—have the hand hold up. It just might, you know. Consider this chain of events in a typical mid-limit hold'em game.

You buy in loud and you buy in big. You post from any-where (because, hell, you're here to gamble, right?). It's folded around to the button, who raises, as buttons will do in most mid-limit games when fresh money comes in. This raise actually does you two favors. First, it defines the raiser's hand as, well, good enough to raise with. Second, it may drop the blinds and leave you heads up against a single player. Now you can strut your stuff! Since you're a Fakiac masquerading as a Mad Cow, you reraise. This puts your opponent back on his heels. He hears all your maniac noise and doesn't necessarily credit you with a good hand, but then again it's possible that you lucked into big cards on your first hand. He may reraise or he may not, but in any case he's now wary. He wanted you to just call, or better yet fold; your raise was not the outcome he desired.

Now here comes the flop. Remember, you're a Fakiac going for the throat, so you don't really care what cards come on the flop. You're going to bet this one according to a program, and the program is this: Check any flop and raise any bet. Again, your goal is to put your opponent off stride. When you check the flop, he assumes that you've missed, and the pot is his for the taking. He can't figure you as tricky enough to check-raise, because he doesn't yet know that you're capable of that. When you *do* check-raise, it has to ring an alarm bell in his head: *The guy could have big cards or big luck; either way, I might be in trouble here.*

You, meanwhile, are talking it up. According to your image (wild or playful or angry or nuts) you're conveying the message that you relish this situation, and you will not be pushed around. The bettor interprets this as white noise designed to disguise a big hand. Thus when you check the turn, he checks too, because he's not about to fall into your check-raise trap twice in a row. Be disappointed. Make it clear that you wanted him to bet. Then bet the river, no matter what it is. If your opponent calls, *do not* slide your cards meekly into the muck. Flip that cheese over. You're a Fakiac. Win or lose, you *want* them to know you play crap.

And if your opponent folds? *Do the same thing!* It's counter-intuitive, I know. No sensible player running a stone-cold bluff would reveal that fact here. But you're not a sensible player right now. You're a Fakiac. You want the maximum bang for your advertising buck, and you won't get that by shipping your tickets to the dealer with a tip-chip on top. The whole point of advertising is to advertise.

From this point forward, continue to be aggressive. Raise where you would normally bet, bet where you would normally check, and check-raise as much as possible. All the while, work to hone your image as someone who is, for whatever reason, *wildly out of control.*

But don't actually *be* wildly out of control. The hands you press with should have some chance of hitting, and give you some leverage if you do hit. That's why 7-8 is a much better Fakiac hand than, say, K-2. Let's not kid ourselves; they're both crappy hands; against a hand such as A-T, they're each about a 2-1 underdog. But the 7-8 plays much better after the flop. Flop a seven or an eight and you have some room to move. Flop a king and you're just asking to get bitch-slapped by all the wheelhouse players in there with K-Q and K-J.

Warning: The Fakiac image is not for everyone! Some players can't pull it off. They don't just seem to be out of line, they *are* out of line, and they'll be punished accordingly. Other players have a gut aversion to lying through image. I don't fault these players, for they're playing their game their way, which is their right. They're just going to war without a full arsenal is all.

Then again, a Fakiac can be as annoying and obnoxious

as a genuine Mad Cow, and it's worthwhile putting your poker play in the context of the greater good. I give you the Law of Conservation of Happiness: If one person is having all the fun, no one else is having any. A Fakiac on a binge may be having a gay old time, but he may be so off-putting to the rest of the table that, basically, he pisses everyone else off. Decide for yourself how much your good karma is worth. To me, it's worth at least something, so that's why my Fakiac plays tend to be out-of-control-jovial, rather than out-of-control-angry.

But I play Fakiac a lot. I do. I look for opportunities to drive cheese holdings into weak opponents, and I look for opportunities to show those hands down. Specifically, if I find myself last to act on the river with, shall we say, an "awkward holding" that has nevertheless emerged as the best hand, I'm not afraid to miss a bet on the end for the sake of displaying my wares. Let's say I raised in late position with 6-3 suited, flopped two pair, and dragged a couple of wheel house hands with me to shakedown street, where it's checked around to me. If I bet I know they'll fold and I won't have to show my cheese. But I *want* to show my cheese. So I check, I show, I put on a show. It's worth a bet or two, it seems to me, for the chance to put a whole table on tilt. And winning with cheese will definitely have that effect.

Will I really raise preflop with 6-3 suited? You bet I will—if the stars are properly aligned. In certain games against certain foes I'm prepared to squander a few bets to establish myself as a lunatic, then sit back and get paid off on good hands for the rest of the night.

What about playing against a Fakiac? What do you do when you're up against someone who seems determined to sell a Mad Cow image but yet betrays an underlying level of awareness or common sense? First detect the difference, then adjust accordingly.

To spot a Fakiac, just watch the eyes. True maniacs rarely

bother to inspect other players, or attend to the play of hands they're not in. If they're genuine buzz junkies they could care less about what other players do or don't do. On the other hand, if they're trying to promote a wild image while still going to school on the rest of the players, their attentiveness will betray them. Disregard the noise; watch the eyes. If "the lights are on and somebody's home," then you know you're up against a Fakiac and not a true Mad Cow.

Next step: Don't buy it! The Fakiac's act is designed to put you on tilt. The Fakiac wants to drag you kicking and screaming out of your comfort zone and put you into a place where you're playing reflexive, reactive hold'em. The Fakiac strives to make you ill at ease by routinely and (seemingly) arbitrarily doubling the size of all bets, betting all flops and turns, putting intense amounts of pressure on you. Perhaps the Fakiac considers you an inferior decision-maker and just wants to put you to a lot of hard choices. Even if you generally make quality decisions, you'll have a tougher time doing so when the Fakiac is calling all the shots.

What to do? Back off. Slow down. Leave the game if necessary, for a game with a skilled Fakiac in it is not favorable to anyone except the Fakiac himself. If you can't leave the game, or choose not to leave the game, just screw down your starting requirements, don your tranquility cap, and wait for the storm to blow over. You can't beat this guy with image and noise (or even hyper-aggressive play) for the simple reason that he's prepared for it and you're not. You beat him by showing down the best hand.

Fakiac will do your betting for you, leaving himself open to trap opportunities. Slow-play your big cards. Check-raise your made hands. Put a couple of beats on the Fakiac and he *will* slow down, at least in relation to you. He'll fig-

ure that you have his number (because you do), that you've
seen through his disguise (because you have), and that his
time and bets are better spent on weaker targets.

At the same time, don't feel the need to tell the Fakiac
that you're on to him. His style of play is, in a sense, a big
fat tell. He's telling anyone smart enough to listen that he
seems to play wild, but *really* plays tight. If he knows that
you have this information, he must necessarily adjust/im-
prove his play, and his improvements will come at your expense. It is required, then, that you blow a little smoke of
your own. If you slow-play a big hand, talk as if you were
afraid to go to war against someone so willing to bet. Make
your snugness, in other words, look like fear, so that the
Fakiac doesn't know you've figured him out.

I like the Fakiac strategy, but it's certainly not the only
way to beat a hold'em game. Sometimes—most of the time—
your standard, solid, no-frills selective-aggressive Killer
Poker will get the job done. On the other hand, in the right
circumstances (for example, a confident player and play-
actor going up against a weak, trainable lineup), Fakiac behavior can pop a game open like a soda can. On the other
other hand, in the wrong circumstances (for example, a
not-quite-committed player going up against savvy and
aware opponents) it's a recipe for self-immolation. To put it
another way, the Fakiac strategy is a powerful force that can
only be used for good or for evil, so always handle with
care!

Thoughtful Joe

I've read a lot of poker books. I own a big
collection. When new ones come out, I usually buy
them. I figure if I get one useful piece of informa-
tion out of any book, it's pretty much paid for

itself. I go back and read certain books in my library over and over again. As the saying goes, "You can't enter the same river twice." The player I was when I read a book the first time is not the player I am when I read it again. Having gained more experience, I glean new insights. Or maybe I just refresh my memory about things I forgot.

I have noticed that a lot of the books contradict one another. You can find hold'em books, for example, that advocate a really wide-open approach to the game, while others lay out start charts and preach your strict adherence. I don't see a conflict there, for I know from my own experience that different hold'em games call for different approaches. Hell, you can see five significant shifts in the nature of a game in one single session, each of which shifts requires an adjustment on your part. So I wouldn't expect to find one-size-fits-all advice in any poker book. Like the man said, "It depends."

I've spent quite a lot of time with hold'em simulators, too. I've investigated situations, because I wanted to see for myself whether a given hand in a given situation against given opponents is worth a fold, call, or raise. These freelance explorations have brought me some startling discoveries. They've made me put a lot less faith in suitedness, for example. When K-Q suited goes up against A-J offsuit, it wins about 44 percent of the time (depending on the exact deployment of suits), but K-Q offsuit, meanwhile, wins about 40 percent of the time. That's a four percent swing, and that's not very much. Rare is the time, if you ask me, when my decision to call or fold rests on a 4 percent fulcrum. Yet when I pick up K-Q suited, I tend to think it's a _much grander hand_ than its offsuit sister. Having run the simulations and seen the numerical evidence with my own eyes, I now know to guard against this subjective overvaluing of suited hands.

While we're on the subject, I know many players who prize a hand like K-Q more highly than, say A-6 or A-2. They reason that they have two hits to win, either the king or the queen, while the A-x holding really has only the ace to count on. They're forgetting, of course, all the times that neither hand pairs, or the times the -x card hits and the king and queen don't. I don't dwell in speculation. I get the facts. Any A-x is better than even money against any K-Q, even suited. Now I'm no longer seduced. I still play my suited K-Q when the situation warrants, but I don't imagine ever that I'm a favorite heads up against an ace. The numbers give me knowledge, and knowledge is power.

I'm not a wonk, though, really. Really, I'm not a wonk. Math is just the starting point for me, When I play hold'em, I pay attention to the texture of the game and spend lots of time and energy getting a psychological read on my foes. I want to know who's soft, who's tilty, who's careless or who, conversely, _came to play_. I'm always on the lookout for focused, disciplined players. They scare me and I try to avoid tangling with them, for I'm humble enough to realize that I'm no favorite over an equally attentive opponent. Hell, when you figure in collection, tokes, and travel, I'm not even break-even. So I dispassionately look for players I know I can dominate. Usually the difference is not in raw skill but in the way that skill is applied. The most skillful player in the world is useless to himself when he's drunk, distracted, bored, angry, tired, or otherwise adrift. That's when I try to attack.

If it seems like I have a pretty level-headed approach to the game, well, yeah, I claim I do. I never go to play unless I feel like I'm bringing my best game with me. I don't play for ego, either, except the ego gratification that comes from expertly applying my knowledge, dedication, and fortitude. I'm into the process of poker. I want to play better today than yesterday. That seems like a goal I can achieve by just doing what I'm doing: reading about poker and thinking about poker and playing poker and using self-awareness to hone my skills and perceptions.

I play for meaningful sums, but I play only with my poker bankroll, and I keep a strong firewall between the money of my life and the money of my game. The last thing I want is to go into some juicy hold'em game knowing that I can't exploit it properly because I'm under-funded or nervous about losing this month's rent. To me that's just crazy. Or no, not crazy: compulsive. Compulsion, I'm happy to say, is a problem I do not have.

Compulsion, I realize, is a problem that many of my hold'em foes do have. I have seen even the best of them hemorrhaging at the wallet, furiously spewing Franklins into games they can't at that moment conceivably beat. I've seen players go on incredible losing jags where they just cease caring how much they lose and seem not to be satisfied or content until they've bottomed out, racked off, gone broke. I've seen dreadful players come back day after day for more punishment, never once recognizing that their total lack of discipline, smarts, or skill dooms them to ruin.

I feel sorry for these people, but not so sorry that I don't want them in my game. I don't have to be reminded that most of my profit comes straight from the mistakes of bad players. I don't have to be told that if I can get certain tilty players' noses open, I can strip-mine their bankrolls and take that money home.

But I don't feel all that good about it when I do.

I know that this empathy is a hole in my game, but I can't help thinking past the compulsive idiot to the people whose lives he's devastating. I feel myself complicit in his act. I don't mind beating a man fair and square, but when his own addictions and limitations are my secret allies, that's _not_ fair and square. That's piling on.

I've had raging debates with myself about this. Part of me says that each of us is responsible for our own actions and decisions, and if someone wants to bring dead money to my hold'em game, how is that my fault? Another part of me has a gut aversion to kicking a man when he's down. These two schools of thought are at war in my mind, and the net result of that conflict is to keep hold'em a secondary interest in my life. I just couldn't feel good about myself if I made my living playing poker, and made that living (as I would have to) at the expense of people too weak-minded to do anything but abet me in their own destruction.

That's not a poker choice, that's a life choice. I don't want it said of me when I die that, "He won more than he lost." That's no legacy for a thoughtful human being.

So I strive (and pretty much succeed, I think) to keep poker in its proper place in my life. I play a lot of hours, and I play those hours with maximum intensity, competitiveness, and joy. I play to win, but win or lose, when I'm done I'm done. I go back to my family, my friends, and my career knowing that I have once again used the recreation of poker appropriately—as a recreation, not as the primary orientation of my life.

At the end of the day I think it's safe to say that poker is really only important to people who have nothing important in their lives.

COMMENT: Thoughtful Joe, I don't mind telling you, is the player I wish I were, not because he's the best, the most dominant, or even the most successful hold'em player in the universe, but because he has his head screwed on so straight. He knows what he's doing, why he's doing it, and how to go about doing it better. I wouldn't fear him in a short-term joust, because he lacks the feral ferocity that the best bully players have, but I'd bet on him to get the money in the long run. He goes about his business.

What can we learn from Joe's approach? First, we can remind ourselves to keep alive our habits of studying and improving our game. As the saying goes, "If you're not slowly getting better, you're slowly getting worse." Joe, by reading and thinking and talking about poker, keeps the accretions of habit from building up around his game. He stays loose, flexible, and informed. And aware. A tremendous strength of Joe's game is his self-awareness. He's honest enough to see his strengths and weaknesses for what they are: parts of his being that, for better or worse, he has to own. I would ask you to take a moment to measure your own level of self-awareness against Joe's, not to judge yourself better or worse than him, but just to know whether you do, in fact, see eye-to-eye with yourself.

Diffidence is Joe's main enemy, and diffidence is the weapon you can use to defeat him. By his own admission, he lacks the killer instinct of a top tier player. He has, if you ask me, way too much sympathy for the mooks from whom his profit comes. And while he seems to care passionately about, as he puts it, "the process of poker," he doesn't seem to care enough about the outcomes. It's one thing to take your losses in stride—we can commend Joe for his tranquility there—but it's another thing to lack grit. I don't see Joe being tough enough to battle the best of the best.

Nor does Joe, and it puts him in a pickle. He says that he avoids messing with superior players, as he should, but he also says he doesn't like to beat up on inferior players too much. Where does that leave him? In the big, fat middle, where play is neither spectacularly good nor spectacularly bad. Day in and day out he can enjoy the joust. He's not going to get broke, but he's not going to get rich either.

A reasonably straightforward player, Joe has trouble with tricky or unpredictable foes. To put him off his game, just throw a little Mad Cow or Fakiac at him. Not only are these roles he's incapable of playing, he has a great deal of difficulty even comprehending them. He's so in control and so self-aware that he can't fathom the mind-set of players who seem determined (or *are* determined) to play heedless, headstrong, hell-for-leather hold'em. His adjustments will be slow in coming, and until he adjusts he will call too many flops and fold too many turns.

But he won't go off for his whole bankroll, not our Joe.

If things aren't going his way, he'll call it a day and go home. This is another strength of his game: He has a home to go home to. Well, we all have homes, be they mansions, Winnebagos, backseats, or cardboard boxes. But Joe has a home away from poker in the broadest existential sense. There are other places in the world where he feels content and happy. That's why he has no trouble walking away from a bad game situation. He's not one of these people who believes that losing at poker is better than not playing poker at all.

Arrogance, as they say, is what confidence wishes it was. Joe lacks arrogance. It's cancelled out by his humility and his honesty. Without this crucial killer ingredient, he can't expect to take his place in the poker pantheon. He seems content not to. He just wants to enjoy his game and improve his skills. We can't begrudge him that, for water finds its level, and Joe seems to have located his.

The Perfesser

I was playing in a tournament the other day. Fixed-limit, headhunter hold'em. At the $100-$200 level, I raised preflop with A-K, got three callers, dropped the blinds, and picked up a beauty flop of A-K-T rainbow. Well, I bet out and two of the players scrammed. That left me alone with just this short-stacker who threw his last chip and his bounty button into the pot. Yum-yum, I thought, I'm gonna get me a bounty, too! We turned over our cards and when I saw that he'd crawled along with just a pair of fours, I really liked my situation. The turn was a brick, but wouldn't you know that the moron spiked a four on the river, stealing the pot—<u>my</u> pot—right out from under my nose.

You can't use the f-word in the tournaments where I play, but there's no law against educating nimrods, so that's what I immediately proceeded to do.

"You _yutz!_" I shouted. "You flaming imbecile! How could you put your case money into the pot against _that_ board?"

"I thought you might be bluffin'," said the muffin.

"Bluffing?! Have you _seen_ me bluff even once? What could I be bluffing with that you could beat? Nine-six? I don't play crap like that and you know it!"

"I had outs," he squeaked defensively.

"Oh, _outs_," I said contemptuously. "You had _outs_. Well, let's just look at those outs, shall we?" I then went on to run the numbers for him, showing him how he was drawing to two outs two times, for about an 8 percent chance of hitting, at a time when the pot was laying him barely 5 to 1. "Not to mention that I could hit an ace or a king, drawing you dead."

"I thought I might get lucky," he said plaintively.

"You had a clear fold!"

"You have to get lucky to win tournaments."

"Yeah, well _you_ do," I snapped, "because you'll never win any other way, I guarantee you that."

He shut up after that and at least I had the satisfaction of knowing that I had made my point. But seriously, there ought to be competency tests for players before you even let them _enter_ these things.

A few hands later I raised on the button with cheese and both of the blinds called. An ace on the flop scared no one, but I bet it anyhow, only to get check-raised. I called down the obvious bluffer, but wouldn't you know—another set! My bounty button went away, and I went home.

Or no, not home exactly. I went over to the $10-$20 ring game, where I discovered that hold'em dimwits are not restricted to tournament tables. After falling victim to some of the most outrageously bad and outrageously lucky play I've ever seen, I'd finally had enough.

Passing the tournament section, I could see that the muffin was still in action, at the final table even, with a big ol' pile of chips. He was having the time of his life.

Guess I smartened him up, huh?

Now look, I don't want you to get the wrong impression of me. I'm a fair guy. I know that everyone has the right to play poker as they see fit. But when they pull such monumental goofs as drawing to two-outers, and when those two-outers steal pots that are rightfully mine, well then they just have to be educated. They have to be set straight.

Dude! Your runner-runner flush draw is a 23-1 shot! Do _not_ draw to it when I've flopped top pair!

Dude! You don't have to defend every blind you play! You can't hit the flop every time, you know!

Dude! _Respect my bets!_ How can you _not_ put me on an ace?! Haven't you been watching me play?

Dude! Look at my great laydown! See how it's done?

Dude! You will never, ever, ever, ever, _ever_ be a winning player playing like that! Go back to keno where you belong!

People say to me, "Hey, Perfesser, maybe you shouldn't give so many lessons at the table. People *don't like being taught to. You're either going to make them play better or get them mad and send them home." You know what I say to that? Kiss my ass! I'm gonna make the dillweeds play correctly if it's the last thing I do! One thing's for sure, I can't beat them until they do.*

Come to think of it, I can't seem to beat them now.

COMMENT: The Perfesser is wrong on so many levels that I almost don't know where to begin. Let's look at the tournament situation that got him so bent out of shape. While it's true that his foe was drawing to two outs twice, for about an 8 percent shot, it's *not* true that the pot was offering him barely 5 to 1. Including the blinds, there was $1050 in the pot when the so-called muffin faced his decision. If muffin had had two chips left, then yes, that would have been about a 5 to 1 call. But muffin had only one chip left, which meant he was looking at an ROI of better than 10 to 1. Adding in the possibility that the Perfesser was bluffing (yes, it happens, Perfesser) and the fact that one chip was not likely to move him much further along in the tournament, the so-called muffin was not so out to lunch as the Perfesser liked to think.

And even if the Perfesser *was* right, why did he open his big yap in the first place?

In a word: pain.

In the moment when that 4 hit the board, the Perfesser took an emotional body blow. Because he's the sort of player who cares more about how he feels than how he plays, the Perfesser needed to make some sort of response, take some sort of action, in an effort to relieve that blast of psychic pain. Other players would curse or throw cards, but because the Perfesser is the Perfesser, he did what he does: He called class to order. His subtext was clear: *By explaining to you what a numbskull you are, I can ease the hurt I feel. By educating you, I get to call you stupid to your face, and somehow that makes me feel better.*

The Perfesser was out of line. Of *course* he was out of line. He was, in fact, out of line at least four different ways. Can you name them?

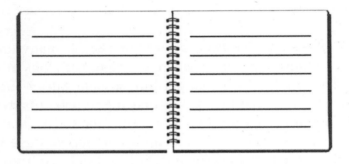

1. By insisting on educating the muffin, he betrayed his own upset, and thus became a target of opportunity for other, cooler, players. His button raise several hands later looked exactly like the tilt-bet it was—and not a soul at the table didn't know it.
2. By educating the muffin, he also *reinforced* his own upset, keeping the pain alive in his mind. From that negative nexus it became impossible to play correctly. All he could think about ... dwell upon ... obsess over ... was how victimized he had been by the other fellow's stupidity.
3. By educating the muffin, he may actually have *educated* the muffin. Could it be that the muffin played more correctly from that point forward (all the way to the final table) because he didn't want to be the object of scorn once again?
4. He was rude. And rudeness is never good for the game.

Does the Perfesser know all this? On some level, yes. Does he care? Not at all. Will he change? Not in a million years. The Perfesser is wired into his worldview. He thinks he's smarter than you, and when your so-called stupidity hurts his outcomes, he gets to feel both superior and persecuted at the same time. It's perversely rewarding, but it's no damn good for his game.

I hate watching the Perfesser do his thing: tapping on the glass; smartening up or scaring off the fish. I find it lamentable. I wish I had the power to change his ways, but nothing short of electro-shock therapy can do that. Nor do I particularly want to make myself the object of his educational excesses. So when the Perfesser is holding forth I usually just hold my tongue. But I take note. I silently take note that here is a target, a big, fat, juicy target, so defined by his own big mouth.

To exploit this target, I just do what the Perfesser hates worse than anything: I play dumb. I present myself as weak and timid and clueless, but really all I'm doing is giving the Perfesser enough rope to hang himself. He will. Sooner or later he'll put that noose right around his neck. Some people never wise up, and the ones telling others to wise up are absolutely the last in line to do so.

Stanley Steemer

Oh, what, I threw a card? Grow up! It's just a card. It's not like I put the dealer's eye out with it. (Though it's not like the dealer doesn't deserve it after rivering me for the third focking hand in a row. What does a focker have to do to make a hand stand up around here?)

Idiots! I am surrounded by focking idiots who don't have the vaguest focking clue how to play this focking game. Did you not see me raise? Did you not credit me with a hand? I haven't been playing shit, you know—or anyway, you <u>would</u> know if you'd been paying the slightest shred of attention, which obviously and manifestly you were not! Next time I'll just turn the focking pocket queens face up so you can know you're beat and get out of the hand. Save you the bets and save me the aggravation.

I mean seriously, what kind of focking jerkweed would call a turn bet when the board is showing 6-9-J-2 rainbow and all he's got is K-8? That's one . . . weak . . . overcard. <u>How can he make that call?</u> And catch a king on the river! Now I'm really focking pissed.

Got to admit, though, I was already kinda focking pissed when I got here today. Bad enough that the tourists plague the Strip with their traffic—now they're clogging up the bails and shortcuts, too. What did they do, focking Mapquest it? They're not supposed to know about Koval Lane. That's <u>my</u> bail. So now I have to wait and wait and wait while all these focking rubbernecking tourists dawdle through the lights. Make a move, you idiot! Johnny on!

I finally get to the cardroom and then it's <u>more</u> wait because the lists are like a mile long and stupid focking floormen don't have the focking foresight to put on enough dealers. Focking casino management is always threatening to rip out the cardroom and replace it with pull toys for the slot monkeys. I wish they would: Put the incompetents who run this lousy room out on the street where they belong.

*Wait and wait and wait and wait and finally,
finally*, I get a seat in a $15-$30 game that
should be half decent if only the focking tumors at
this table were smart enough to know how focking
stupid they are. Don't take that draw, you numb-
nuts! Can't you see you have the worst of it? No?
Okay, fine, then—river me again. What else is
focking new?

I could kill 'em, your honor, no jury would
convict. I have kings, they flop an ace. I have
aces, they've got two pair. I flop a straight, they
turn a flush. I turn a flush, they river a boat. And
does it ever go the other way? No! Never focking
ever! Think about this: I'm in the big blind
with 8♠-7♠. By some incredible miracle no one
raises my blind and I get a flop of A♠-6♠-5♦.
I'm no idiot, I know the numbers. I know I've
got 15 outs. I'm odds on to hit my hand, but
do you think I could hit a favorite *just focking
once?*

No wonder I throw cards.

All I want is justice, judge. There's no focking
justice in the world.

Oh, and then the whiners say I bring it on
myself with my "bad attitude." Give me a focking
break. I'm not superstitious. I know about
independent events. I know that a smiley face or a
frowny face can't determine which cards come off
the deck.

Dealers do that.

And the dealer just did it again, to my pocket
aces, by spewing a harmless-looking 6-6-2 out
across the board so some flathead screwdriver
could call me down with 6-9 offsuit that he only

played because—as he says with a focking giggle—
"sixty-nine is oh so fine."

Fock!

Focking focking focking fock!

Floorman?! Now you're calling the floorman?!
What, because I said fock? I said fock, not fuck,
you fock. Clean out your ears, earwax. You hear as
bad as you play.

You think I should calm down? Okay, fine, I'll
calm down. There, I'm calm, see? The Sea of focking Tranquility. But don't think I'll forget what
happened, chuckles. Don't think I won't raise
your blind every focking time it comes around
because I focking will. I don't care what I've got.
I can win with bottom pair too, you know. Oh,
you've got top pair, top kicker? Fock, how did that
happen?

Chips! Chips on two!

It's gonna be a long focking night.

COMMENT: Poor Stanley Steemer, he was steaming before he even sat down. By his own admission he was steaming in traffic, but I suspect that he started steaming even
earlier, just as soon as he started thinking about coming
into the cardroom, a place he has come to see as a veritable
black hole of injustice. He's got to play because he's been
running bad and he needs to turn that around. But he hates
to play because he dreads the torment he considers inevitable.

Stanley's caught in a nasty little negative feedback loop.
We're familiar with this loop already, but let's examine
Stanley's version:

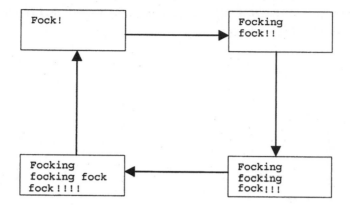

Stanley embodies the expression *To an asshole, the whole world looks dark*. His contempt for himself and his foes and for life in general sends him spiraling down into a vortex of self-fulfilling prophecy. He expects the worst, so he plays all stressed and angry, makes poor decisions, and gets bad outcomes, which reinforces his cherished belief that he's justified in expecting the worst. Nothing worse in this world than a justified resentment, and Stanley has his in bunches.

He resents the other players. He resents the dealers and the floor personnel; the chip runners and cocktail waitresses, too. He resents people who walk too slowly in front of him when he's on a between-hands bathroom dash. He resents the woman whistling at the next table because why is *she* so damn happy? He resents smokers. He resents non-smokers. He resents when he loses. He resents when he wins. He resents, to quote the man himself, "All the focking time."

Stanley is an extreme case, but to truth to tell, there's a little bit of Stanley in me. I know of at least a few resentments I can own.

I resent the sweaty guy sitting next to me for having B.O. I resent angle shooters. I resent people who ask for deck

*changes. I resent dealers who don't pay attention. I resent
poker buddies who soft play each other.*

How about you? Do you harbor a hold'em resentment
or two? Are you brave enough to cop to them?

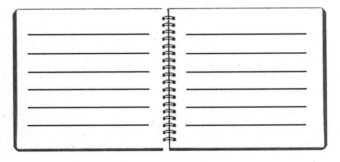

A guy like Stanley is, of course, a vulnerable mark. You
don't even have to work that hard at unraveling him, since
he's so busy unraveling himself. If you're looking for a
moral justification for taking this sort of player apart, you
might tell yourself that anyone who brings that much bad
karma to the table deserves what he gets. I don't really
think justification is necessary, though. He's here of his
own free will. No one held a gun to his head and made him
put his money in play.

Right, then, how can we take his money away?

One trick is to aim speculative raises his way. In situations where you're adding some deception to your play by
raising with middle suited connectors, try to make those
raises directly against Stanley, either into his blind or after
he's limped. His righteous indignation is always primed
and ready to blow. When you raise with an off-center hand
that runs over his pedestrian wheelhouse holding, it reinforces his cherished belief that people are punishing him—
him, specifically—with inferior play and blind luck. This

will make him play worse and worse, as his anger simmers and brews.

Am I talking about putting him on tilt? Damn right I am! He's so close to tilt anyhow—by his very nature—that virtually any (perceived) bad beat will light the fuse and send him into space. This is the extra mileage that we get out of our so-called "bad raises." Many is the time I'll bump it with 9♦-8♦—and many is the time I have to surrender that hand on the flop. But when it gets there, when it gets under the skin of a steamer, it pays dividends that will last as long as that player has chips.

Trapping is also useful against Stan because he often gets out ahead of his hand. He's a steamer, don't forget. In the name of getting even all at once, he'll play his A-J or A-T full throttle. That's the time to decelerate your A-Q or A-K. Let Stanley do your work for you. If the flop comes ace-little-little, he'll think he's golden. What happens next is painfully predictable. He bets the flop and you call. He bets the turn and you raise. He calls your raise, and calls again on the river, because he's damned if he'll let himself get focked with by a twerp like you. Then he fumes when you show down the quality hand that you nefariously slow-played.

This sequence of events has the added benefit of *explosive defeat of expectation*. Having hit an ace on the flop, and not encountered a raise, Stanley was already building the expectation of winning the pot. He bets on the turn, probably expecting you to fold like a good little girl or boy. When you raise, his world is turned upside down. In an instant he goes from confident driver to shocked and sullen victim. For someone prone to taking every setback way too personally, this explosive defeat of expectation can be just devastating. He erupts. He tilts. He's history.

On the next hand, he raises from pure venom. You reraise, completing your pre-planned one-two punch. He's afraid of you. You flat-called with A-K; you must have A-A or K-K now. If he were thinking clearly, he'd figure out that you're much more likely to be bluffing than to have a real hand here. But he's not thinking clearly because he's Stanley Steemer, so he throws away his hand and, growling, sits back to lick his wounds.

Do you turn over the 9-2 you raised with?

I would.

But also have a security guard walk me to my car.

Mighty Aphrodite

People call me fearless when I play hold'em, but I honestly don't know what they're talking about. What's there to be afraid of in hold'em? Losing money? It's not even money. It's just chips, round colored pieces of plastic. Fear that? Not in this lifetime.

Oh, I know, I know, the chips represent money. You can convert them into cash when you're done, and if you lose them all then you can't convert them into anything and you have to go home broke, poor you. I can see how people feel that way, but I'm sorry, I just don't.

People also call me relentless when I play, and that's a title I can own. Just because I enjoy my poker doesn't mean I don't take it seriously, and just because I don't fear losing doesn't mean I don't want to win. When I sit down to play I give it everything I've got: my brains, my skill, my experience, my intuition, and my heart. Especially my heart. I've got a lot of gamble in me, and I come by it naturally. In some families, kids are taught not to risk; they're taught to play it safe. In my family, we were taught, hey, you can't win if you don't play, and you have to risk big to win big. That's an attitude that goes back in my family for as long as anyone can remember. Generations. Eons! We probably emerged from the primordial ooze with dice in one hand and chips in the other.

I like the big win. I like walking out of the casino saying, "Yeah, I did that. I _ruled_ that game." I don't find it that hard to do. For some reason, playing hold'em is something I just naturally do quite well. Whenever I join a game I figure I'm probably gonna be the best player at the table, and I'm usually not wrong. Though you wouldn't think so to look at me. Young as I am, baby-faced (and not unattractive), you wouldn't suspect that I have this savage streak in me, but I do. I'm like a shark. I move in for the kill.

When someone I don't know sits down at the table, my first thought is, "Well, let's see what he's made of." Then I engage . . . I _attack_. I'm used to seeing other players back down, so used to it that it becomes predictable. I raise, they call. I bet the flop, they call. I bet the turn, they fold. Moving right along . . .

I win a lot of these fold-outs, pots where all the callers surrender to me on the flop or the turn. It's almost laughable, really. I come on so strong with my betting that they don't know where I'm at, and they're reluctant to commit a lot of money to their ignorance. I also win with good cards, 'cause people pay me off. And if I don't think I can run a bluff, I just check. Since people know how fearless I am, they're afraid to bet into me, lest I check-raise. I get way more than my share of free cards. Best of both worlds, right? I get to bet when I think I'm gonna win (either by bluffing or by having a hand) and I don't have to bet when I'm beat. Why? I don't know. That's just the way I play, and the way people seem to respond.

I'm tricky by nature. I slow-play good hands and fast-play bad ones. I raise and reraise a lot. I check-raise a lot. I check-raise <u>bluff</u> a lot, and that's a hard move to pull off. My image helps me there; my baby face. They just can't believe I don't have the goods.

They really don't think I know what I'm doing.

I don't know how I got so good. I don't remember ever being terribly bad. I started out small, like everybody does, but it seemed like only a heartbeat before I was dancing up the limits: $2-$4, $3-$6, $6-$12, $10-$20, $30-$60, $100-$200. These days I play as high as I can find. Big tournaments too, and I've won more than a few. I've got it going on.

I've never read a poker book in my life. I've never seen the need. I'm not being cocky in saying that, I'm just telling it like it is. Nor have I ever studied the math of the game, but I always seem to know where I'm at with the odds. How do I know? I don't know, I just <u>know</u>. Like some people can hit a baseball or play music by ear, I play hold'em from the inside out. It doesn't work for everyone, but it sure does work for me.

I know when my hand is good. I know when my opponents are on draws. I know when they're strong and I know when they're bluffing. Do I have tells on them? Not consciously, not that I'm aware of. It's just a vibe they give off, something I'm sensitive to. Sometimes, not all the time, I have a read so strong they might as well be playing their cards face-up. A friend says I have ESP, but that's bullshit. I don't believe in ESP. I believe in nuance. A twitch or a hitch in your hand when you bet . . . that's meaningful as hell to me, in ways I can't begin to describe. On my best days you give yourself away to me completely, and there's nothing you can do.

Do I make my living playing poker? You bet your ass I do. I made a quarter of a million dollars last year playing poker. And that's not anecdote money; that's taxable earnings and tournament wins, rigorously recorded and scrupulously tracked. I'm not one of these phony baloney pro manqués who tell you they earn 1½ big bets per hour, but really they're lucky if they can beat the drop for a dime.

People can't believe how lucky I am. I agree that I'm lucky, but not in the way that they mean. I'm not particularly lucky in terms of the cards that I get. I'm very lucky in terms of being able to use them well. In a larger sense, I'm lucky that I can make a living doing something I love. But I once heard someone say that you'd better love what you do, because if you don't love it you won't do it well. Maybe that's where it begins and ends for me: I love playing hold'em, so therefore I do it well—or I do it well, so therefore I love it. Either way, I can't wait to see what the next hand brings.

COMMENT: Here we have a genuinely gifted poker player. She sees the game on an intuitive level that is, frankly, beyond the reach of most run-of-the-mill players' perceptions. Is it conditioning, genetics, cultural background, family upbringing, or God-given genius? Probably all of the above. Her cultural background and family upbringing have freed her from fear. It's not that she can tolerate risk better than others. Rather, risk is invisible to her. She doesn't see putting money, even big money, in play as a risky business in any sense at all. No wonder she plays aggressively and makes unexpected moves with surprise holdings and presses thin edges and bluffs bluffers and a host of other sophisticated plays. In her mind *she has nothing to lose*. Wouldn't you play that way if you had nothing to lose?

Wedded to this fearlessness is an innate sense of the game. Aphrodite says she's never read a poker book, and I believe her. She is no more aware of poker theory than a fish is aware of the ocean. She merely inhabits the game, but she inhabits it so thoroughly and organically that she's just unstoppable. And, again, she doesn't consider being stopped as *losing*. To her, there is no such thing as winning or losing. There's just the game, and the game goes on forever.

Can skills such as hers be learned or taught? That's a matter of opinion, and you might ask Antonio Salieri for his. Salieri, would-be mentor to, and jealous admirer of, Wolfgang Amadeus Mozart, always wanted what Mozart had— the unself-conscious talent; the effortless ease at composing memorable music. Salieri struggled to make his own music technically correct, and much of it was pleasing to the ear. But it lacked that certain je ne sais quoi, the x factor that separates competent work from works of genius. In this life, it seems to me, you're either a Mozart or a Salieri, and if you're a Salieri of hold'em, the best you can do is hone your craft and stay out of the Mozarts' way.

If you find yourself in a situation where you can't run for cover (at a tournament table, for example), there are a couple of adjustments you can make to minimize the damage an Aphrodite can do to your stack. First (and this is hard for many people) *admit that you're outclassed.* There's no shame in acknowledging (to yourself at least) that another player has superior skills. The only real shame is in denying this fact to the detriment of your efforts to win. So start by saying, "Well, this is a really terrific player. I'm going to have to watch my step."

This doesn't mean you should run scared. Fear helps nobody's game. But you ought to be cautious, and you should avoid confrontations with any enemy whose combination of dominant skills, deep insight, and utter fearlessness adds up to an edge you can't overcome with cards alone. At the end of the day, though, cards are really the only weapon you can trust. Raise less, trap more, and tighten up your starting requirements. By doing these things, you will present the smallest possible target to this admittedly superior player.

I'd like you to spend a moment with your memory and recall a time when you found yourself locked in battle with someone you knew to have the best of you. What adjustments did you make? How did they pan out? And how did it make you feel to have to make such adjustments?

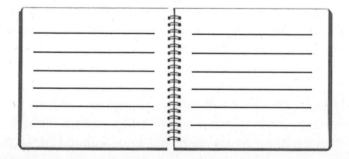

In the presence of truly gifted players who crowd our action and cramp our style, average players have predictable reactions. We become jealous and aggravated. If we're not careful, we get angry or agitated or feel threatened, and let our egos drive our decisions. Then we get involved in confrontations we can't win. Losses result, setbacks happen, and sorrow ensues.

How does Aphrodite feel about all this? Does she enjoy watching her opponents crumble, or does she feel sorry for the lesser lights? The truth is, she probably doesn't even know we're there. We're just chess pieces that she's moving around the board. No wonder we feel belittled.

Poker is a continuum of knowledge, experience, talent, and skill. Each of us is somewhere along the continuum. Some foes are behind us. Others are ahead. Except as a strategic consideration—*is this a player I can beat?*—there's no sense in getting involved in this measuring shtick. Accept that a player is better than you and deal with her accordingly. Above all, *watch her intently*, because against this foe you'll need every scrap of edge you can get, and the utility of any tell you capture from such a player will be magnified by her own dominating presence in the game. Even if you can't catch a tell, you can always gain insight into how a terrific player plays. Her approach to the game is a model you can study and learn from and use to improve your own play. Salieri never had what Mozart had, but that didn't stop him from being the best damn Salieri he could be. I hope that was enough for him.

Let's hope it's enough for us.

Though we've looked at some familiar hold'em archetypes, there are many that we haven't considered yet. I can think of a few: *the Fossil; the Hotshot; the Sexpot; Stranger from the East; Good Time Charlie; Jackpot Jackie; Eyes Wide Shut; Drunky Tilty; Joe Btfsplk (the world's unluckiest man); Granny Bifocals; Goodle Boy.*

I imagine that you can think of a few, too.

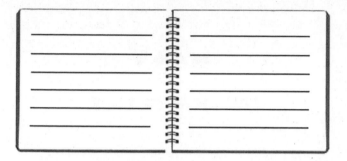

Now here comes a challenge, and I hope you're up to it. Take one or two of these unexplored archetypes and explore them. Write down or at least jot down (or at least thoroughly think through) some of your observations. Nothing will help you see your own game more clearly than to see the game you play through the eyes of someone else.

4

♣ ♠ ♦ ♥

INNER GAME

♧ ♤ ◇ ♡

Hold'em, as a whole, is the sum of its parts. The amount of money you win in a year is a function of the amount you win each month. Your monthly totals reflect your weekly performance. Your weekly performance gets built on a platform of daily sessions, with each session having its own hands, flops, bets, and choices. In a very real sense, then, your overall bottom line depends specifically and exactly on how you play your bad aces, what you do with middle pocket pairs, whom you bluff and when, and countless other recurring parts of the game.

In this section we'll look at some of these recurring parts, and examine the sort of choices you can make and the kind of thought that should go into those choices. By this point in our work together, I trust I can assume that your choices are based on a clear-eyed appraisal of the situations you find yourself in, and not skewed by unrealistic hope, undue fear, irrelevant machismo/a, or psychic pain. Having well surveyed the length and breadth of the hold'em canvas, we're now ready to delve into the inner game.

LPOP

LPOP stands for "little pairs out of position." Let's take a look at them and see how the play of them can be a seductive loser, a leak in our games that we can stand to plug. For the sake of this discussion, we'll define *little pairs* as anything below pocket eights, and *out of position* as anywhere from under the gun to middle position.

When you play LPOP, you're hoping for an outcome parlay; that is, you need a number of related outcomes to occur. Here's everything you're hoping for.

1. You get sufficient callers.
2. You face no raises.
3. You flop a set.
4. Your hand holds up.

Let's examine each of these parlay parts in turn.

You're under the gun with 4-4. Since you're looking to hit a set on the flop, your 7.5-1 shot certainly needs a bunch of customers to justify the call. In a perfect world, you'll limp in and have a full field limp in behind you. But realistically, in what kind of hold'em game do you consistently see seven smooth callers and no raisers? So you look beyond the initial odds to implied odds. You figure that on subsequent rounds you'll make enough money to justify your initial call. Oh, really? Suppose everyone drops but the small and big blinds. Now you're getting a 2-1 ROI on a 7.5-1 shot. That won't change. If you hit your set, you'll collect more bets on later streets, but you'll only accrue them at the same 2-1 rate—or less if one of your opponents folds. And you must make this calculation based on hitting your set on the flop only, not on the turn or river, since if you miss the flop and face any heat at all, you're going to have to let the hand go.

So here's the first danger of LPOP. You need a lot of callers, and you have to make your own commitment before you know whether you're going to get them or not. If you have a solid read on the players downstream—if you know them to be loose and passive—you may be able to predict the outcome you need. That is, you may know them to be prepared to call, and not raise, with unpaired wheelhouse cards. But what if they're holding better than that? Don't forget, in a full game an average of two hands will have a pair or an ace. Which brings us to the second point in our parlay: *They might raise.*

Suppose you limp with your 4-4 and someone raises behind you. In the best of circumstances, the raiser is frisky and out of line, and all the callers are loose and clueless. For example, someone raises with A-2 offsuit and a lot of people call two bets cold with hands like Q-2 suited and T-8 offsuit. Get that kind of outcome and you can probably justify throwing in another bet of your own. But how can you count on that kind of outcome? Raises don't mean nothing, and cold-calls don't mean nothing. Downstream action of this sort is self-selecting: It defines your opponents' hands as the type that might very well dominate your own. Granted, against A-K, you're about even money, but against any bigger pocket pair, you'll lose roughly 80 percent of the time.

A typical single-raise situation would likely look like this: You flat-call in early position with 4♣-4♦. Someone raises behind you with T♠-T♦. A J♣-Q♣ calls, as does an A♥-9♥. The small blind folds, but the big blind calls with 8♦-7♦. How do you like your pocket fours now? Against this exact field, you'll win a whopping 15 percent of the time—*and that's only if you hit a four on the flop,* because, again, if you miss on the flop you probably can't go further into the hand.

The seductive menace here is how attractive the pot looks when you're called upon to call a single raise. Suppose the person to your left raises and there are four callers (including both blinds) by the time it gets back to you. You'd be putting a single small bet into a pot containing 11 small bets. Who doesn't like 11-1 odds, right? That's an overlay to your 7.5-1 odds against hitting your set on the flop. You should be in business, right?

Wrong. Your total preflop contribution to this pot is *two* small bets, for a 5-1 ROI against a 7.5-1 shot. You wouldn't be faced with this "favorable" call if you hadn't made a mistake in the first place. There's a technical phrase for this circumstance. It's called *throwing good money after bad*. By promiscuously playing LPOP, you've maneuvered yourself into a situation where calling the raise seems like a good investment, but viewed in the context of the hand as a whole, it is not.

In short, if there's a reasonable chance of a real hand making a real raise behind you, your little pairs out of position become an untenable proposition.

But what if you hit parts one and two of your parlay? Suppose you've gotten a lot of callers and no raisers. Though you're seeing the flop under the most favorable possible circumstances, you still need to hit to win. Ideally, you'll hit a flop like A-K-4 and get paid off by all those naked aces and kings. Or maybe the flop will come 4-9-T. This flop gives you plenty of room to move. You can check, hoping that someone behind you will bet with middle pair, good kicker, or even bluff into your stealthy set. Then you can check-raise, either here or on the turn or river, and maximize your advantage of flopping a set.

More often—much more often—you'll find yourself staring at a fourless flop like A-J-6 or 7-8-8. Now you have *no* wiggle room. All you can do is check, fold if they bet, and minimize your loss on the hand. And that's the choice you'll face almost 90 percent of the time. But you still have two outs, right? You could hit a four on the turn or the river, and in many circumstances that would be a winning hand.

Once again, a rough calculation of the odds can be a Siren's song to further involvement. Driven by the desire to see this thing through, we add our pot odds and our implied odds, plus our frequent flier miles, buffet comps and time off for good behavior and, lo and behold, we almost have a call. Assuming we need a 4 to win, and assuming that a 4 *will* win, we have two outs two times, roughly 8 percent, and if we've gotten six preflop and six post-flop callers to put 13 small bets into the pot, why, that's all the pot odds we need.

In what kind of fantasyland do we get six preflop and six post-flop callers without any of them (or *many* of them) slow-playing made hands or else drawing fat? We're working *so hard* to finesse the numbers to the point where we don't lose money on the hand—a circumstance we'd have had for sure if we just hadn't called in the first place. And that's really the point here: More often than not, LPOP digs us into a hole we could have avoided by just laying down that hand at the start.

But, hey, dreams do come true, right? So let's say we got lots of calls and no raises preflop, and then flopped a delightful 4-8-Q rainbow. We don't put anyone on pocket queens because we'd have heard about that before the flop. And when we bet and no one raises, we figure that pocket 8s aren't out against us either. Now all we have to do is survive the turn and the river, and we can bring this bad boy home.

We sure hope no one is in there with J-T, drawing to an inside straight, because if a 9 hits we'll have to pay it off.

But J-T is exactly the sort of hand we hoped would call preflop.

We sure hope no one is in there with Q-8, because then a queen or an 8 would murder us with a bigger full house.

But Q-8 is exactly the sort of hand we hope will stick around.

We sure hope no one is in there with a pair of 5s, seducing themselves into drawing to two outs.

But 5-5 is exactly the sort of hand we hope will continue to call to the river.

Yes, our set of 4s is a big favorite against any of these holdings. It's even a slight favorite against all three taken together. But look how many excellent outcomes we need in order to reach this advantageous spot: loose, weak play preflop; a perfect flop; and now many opponents making many mistakes between here and the river. Oh, and not sucking out. If everything breaks our way, our four-part parlay comes through and we win the pot.

What an uphill climb.

If you never call with LPOP, then this discussion doesn't apply to you. But if you *do* call, if you ever *have* called, ask yourself why. It's not a favorable situation, and you probably knew it wasn't a favorable situation before this labored deconstruction. Could it be that you just wanted the action? Could it be that you picked up a little pair and thought about how good you'd feel if your hand hit? It's been that way for me—more times than I can count. Moral of the story: Even the most conscious and conscientious players let their feelings guide their choices from time to time. It's human nature. It's why we play cards in the first place.

And it's why I take such pains to analyze the play of LPOP. So that the next time I pick up a small pair under the gun, I'll have a weapon to use against that desire to *just feel good*. I'll have a painful scenario to remind me that the best thing I can do, most of the time, is just slide that pair in the muck.

Look, I'm not a fan of hard and fast rules. We all know

that the words "it depends" inform any hold'em analysis. But how much trouble could you get into if you never played little pairs out of position? Do you honestly think your win rate would go down? At least try this: For your whole next session, throw away every LPOP you see, and see how that makes you feel.

It might make you feel all the good you need.

RECKLESS ADVENTURES

Go long enough between starting hands and you start looking for a reason to end inaction and get involved. Sit on your thumbs long enough and you'll eventually get all moist and juicy over something like A♥-4♥, and decide to bring it in for a raise. Maybe you'll think, *it's been so long since I've played a hand that everyone must figure me for supertight. Therefore, if I raise here, they're bound to put me on a big pocket pair and let me win in a walk.* Well, that's one scenario. Here's another: They see your inaction not as tightness but timidity. Now when you come in for a raise, they're licking their lips and planning to bet you off your hand. This deadly combination—your impatience, plus a foe's pugnacious misinterpretation of your action—can drop you spang-blam into the middle of a reckless adventure.

You raise with that weenie suited ace and it's folded around to someone in late position who reraises. It's folded back to you. Already you don't like your choices.

You could fold, but if you do you're just asking to be played with exactly the same way on your next adventure.

You could call, and hope to hit a flop you can bet . . . out of position against a foe who's representing a hand strong enough to reraise with.

Or you could raise him back, and *really* get out ahead of your hand.

Let's assume the worst. Let's assume that you're outclassed by your opponent and you know it. The prudent thing to do would be to fold now—*oops, my bad!*—and let him have the pot. The bold thing to do would be to raise back—*take that!*—and send the message that you're willing to go to war. The typical thing to do would be to meekly call the re-raise—*what the hell!*—and hope for a favorable flop.

The trouble is, you don't know if your foe has a real hand or not. If he is who you think he is—a wily and fearless player—he could have anything at all or nothing at all. You have to hit to win, but he doesn't. Not only does he have the higher ground—position—he controls most flops. Anything that doesn't come rich in aces, 4s, abundant other wheel cards, or hearts misses your hand, and could very well hit his. Even if you do hit an ace, you can't feel too frisky because any ace he holds is likely to be better than yours. So you're looking specifically to flop two pair or a flush draw. Good luck with that.

In most cases, you'll see flops that don't fit your hand. How will you proceed? If you check, your aggressive foe is sure to bet, inviting you to minimize your loss and fold now. This sort of surrender may be prudent, but it does nothing for your table image or future prospects. Is there another option? Maybe.

When I find myself in this situation—and yes, of course I find myself in this situation; you think you're the only one who goes out on reckless adventures?—I start looking for certain types of flops that I can use to take away the pot. I'm expanding my outs, so to speak, to include not just legitimate hit-outs but also legitimate *bluff-outs*. Specifically, I'm looking for a flop that's either trappy or coordinated.

A trappy flop is something like T-T-7. I check. My foe bets. I call. Then, almost no matter what the turn is (but especially if it's something bricky like a deuce) I'm going to go ahead and bet out. I want my opponent to conclude that I'd started out preflop by overbetting (in my impatience) something like A-T, or K-T or J-T suited, flopped three of a kind, and check-called the flop to extract maximum value. I'm hoping that my big bet on the turn will cause him to make what he considers a smart laydown.

With a coordinated flop, something like J-9-8 or three to a suit, I'm going to check-raise the flop, making what looks like a standard foreclosure raise designed to buy a free card on the turn. Here I'm representing a naked 10 or a single high card suited to the board. I need a scare card on the turn, but there are eight or nine of them in the deck at this point, and these are my so-called bluff-outs.

Does this sort of "program bluffing" work? It can, against the right foe. It'll work against a Fakiac, for instance, because the Fakiac has both aggressiveness (motivating his preflop reraise) and common sense (motivating his laydown on the turn). He's thoughtful enough and disciplined enough to get away from his hand. Most opponents are not, so, as with any bluff attempt, you have to pick your spots.

You need an opponent who plays according to *self-interest*, someone who will draw the conclusion you want him to draw and get away from his hand. You don't want an opponent who plays according to *self-image*, for this foe doesn't care about losing bets, but only about losing face. There are plenty of self-image players out there though, and once they've gotten involved in one of these shooting wars, they're not likely to back down. They'll call you on the turn, call again on the river, and snap off your bluff—which will reinforce their preflop strategies and make them that much harder to beat later on.

In this sort of confrontation, the player who never folds has a certain advantage over us sensible we-know-when-we're-beaten types. He can win the pot two ways: He can

have the best hand, or he can make us flinch. We, on the
other hand, can never make him flinch. If he's fold-proof,
he's flinch-proof. He may lose some bets and he may lose
some pots, but he won't lose to a bluff. He'll call us down
because, in a sense, we've called him out. He simply will
not blink.

The program bluff, then, is at best an emergency escape
route from a reckless adventure. It would be so much better
if we never got involved in this reckless adventure in the
first place. Is it really so hard to be patient? Is it really so
hard to look at A♥-4♥ and see the kind of trouble it can get
you into? If it *is* that hard, could it be that your problem is
overall discipline and not the specific play of hands?

In a weak-tight game, when you're running good and
your image is strong, A-4 suited is a perfectly raiseworthy
hand—but so is 2-7 offsuit, because *you are in control.* When
you're running the table, when you're not the one who has
to hit to win, when it's the other guys who flinch, you can
play virtually any cards. But if you've been dormant for a
long time because the cards haven't been running your
way, you need to be very selective about the hands with
which you choose to re-announce yourself to the table.
Strong, smart players will be waiting like snipers, planning
to pop you the minute you stick your head up.

I can think of some other reckless adventures. I wonder
if you can, too. Here are a couple I'm guilty of:

*Everyone checks a flop of K-x-x. On the turn, the player
first to act bets out. I'm next, and I raise with nothing, trying to bluff out not only the raiser (who may have checked
a weak king on the flop) but everyone behind me as well.*

*I'm on the button, holding A-x offsuit. I'm prepared to
raise if nobody opens, but someone in middle position does*

open, getting a couple of calls. I call anyhow, hoping to hit, I suppose, two pair on the flop.

I get involved in raising wars with maniacs just 'cause they cheese me off.

And here are a couple you have launched:

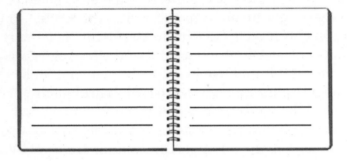

Know your foes. Know yourself. Recognize that the need for action and involvement can draw anyone into reckless adventures. All other things being equal, let the other guy have them instead.

CLEAR GESTALT

When I enter a new game, I hate starting play on the big blind because I'm in bad position.

When I enter a new game, I hate starting play by posting behind the button because I'm putting extra blind money in the pot and inviting aggressive play.

When I enter a new game, I hate buying the button because I'm putting absolutely dead money (the small blind) into the pot in absolutely the worst position.

When I enter a new game, I . . .

Well, it looks like I sort of hate entering a new game under any circumstances. And hey, you know what? I do. On that first hand, no matter where or how I post, I'm the new blood, the fresh meat, the one that *someone* is bound to test. Not only that, if I get raised (usually at the limits I play it's more a case of *when* I get raised) I often haven't played against the bettor before, and don't know whether he raises with true value or with speculative holdings or with nothing at all. In this case, you might say that I'm in a double-blind bind. Not only was my post a blind bet, my play of the hand must perforce be blind because I just don't know my foes.

But who likes to give up without a fight, right? I know that new players routinely get played with, so I'm tempted to call that raise with my K-9 or little string cheese. I don't want people to think they can push me around, so I often defend first hands that I'd never defend in the normal flow of the game. I'm hoping to flop lucky and start my session off on the right foot. But I'm still playing the hand blind. How stupid am I?

No stupider than most, I guess, just overly focused on something that doesn't really matter. Who cares if the first hand is a win or a loss? Aren't I in this for the long haul? Don't I care more about playing correctly throughout the session than about any individual outcome? Of course I do—in my head. But in my gut . . . no. I don't want people to push me around. I don't want to be forced to fold, but I also don't want to get into a reckless adventure and end up starting the session a whole stack back instead of just two or three or four chips. I hate all my options. What the hell am I going to do?

It seems to me that there are two things I can do. I can change my strategy, or I can change the way I feel.

In the case of strategy, I might consider getting into the

habit of responding to that first attack against me by reraising with a wide range of hands, thus taking control of the hand and/or creating bluffing opportunities for myself. I might still lose, but at least I won't lose passively. Of course, I'm still going up against unknown opponents, and aggressive moves always work better when you know how your foes will respond.

So, no, I'm not going to go all postal when I post. I'm still going to call with callworthy hands, raise with raiseworthy ones, and throw the rest away. I'm not going to make a precipitous and unwarranted play adjustment. I'll make an *attitude* adjustment instead.

I have some experience in this area.

Years ago, when my wife and I first moved to Los Angeles, we had trouble adjusting to the—shall we say—"imaginative habits" of L.A. drivers. Every day we'd see people running red lights, making right turns from left-hand lanes, flying solo in the carpool lane, speeding, tailgating, passing on the right, and on and on. These reckless bad drivers made us angry every time we went out driving. We knew we had to make a change. So we decided that whenever we saw someone driving "L.A. style," we'd put a couple of bucks in a kitty in the car. "The bucket," we called it. Soon, we found ourselves no longer ruing the L.A. drivers, but actually rooting for them to misbehave. We'd see someone bearing down on a stale yellow light and we'd yell, "Go! Go! Go!" And then when they ran the light we'd shout, "Yes! Two dollars in the bucket!" If you've ever driven in L.A., you won't be surprised to learn that the bucket fills up fast. When the bucket gets full enough, we take ourselves out to dinner or to a nice hotel for the night.

Self-delusion, right? After all, it's all our money to begin with. It's not like it's doing anything but going from one pocket to another. Nothing has changed. Nothing, that is, except our attitude. We've taken something that made us feel bad and turned it into something that makes us feel good. I have a friend, a magazine journalist, who does a similar trick with rejection letters. No writer likes rejection letters, of course, but this guy takes all of his and wallpapers his bathroom with them. Bad news in the mail is still bad news, but it's also help with a household project and part of a game he plays.

I seek to play the first hand of a hold'em session the same way. Instead of looking at it as a source of frustration or annoyance or threat (or even as a source of opportunity, which, since I'm up against unknown foes, it's probably not) I simply view it as something I have to get through before I get down to the serious business of taking over the table. A tax, if you will, or an entry fee to the game.

Sometimes, in my playfulness, I'll post my blind bet and then just walk away. Of course someone is going to bet me off my hand, but they won't have *scared* me off, will they? If nothing else, I've established an unpredictable, or even a lunatic, image. I've established it strongly and persuasively and immediately, and it hasn't cost me anything but a single forced blind bet that I'll usually have to sacrifice anyhow. If I sit down and play that post seriously, I can establish nothing but a serious image. I can establish myself only as someone who defends his first hand incorrectly, which is not so good—or else correctly, which is not much better. The way I see it, if I'm going to have to flush a bet anyhow, I might as well get some image muscle out of it. I never mind being thought of as insane; it's an image that works for me.

What I'm really doing, though, is looking past the first hand and, in fact, past the first few dozen hands, to that point in the session where I can start to take control. What I'm looking for, what I've come to expect, is something I call the *clear gestalt,* the moment in a hold'em contest when I suddenly figure everything out.

Gestalt, by the way, is "a unified whole; a configuration, pattern, or organized field having specific properties that cannot be derived from the summation of its component parts." In a poker context this doesn't mean knowing that seat one is lemmy or seat six check-raises flush draws or seat nine is scared to lose. It means knowing *all of it:* understanding all the players and all their plays, all taken as a whole. I have discovered that I will usually achieve this understanding—I will enter the realm of the clear gestalt— if I only do two simple things:

1. Wait.
2. Pay attention.

Yes, it's a shocking notion, but I have reason to believe that it's true. All I have to do to win is *wait* and *pay attention.* Given enough time, watching enough hands, sooner or later I'll enter the clear gestalt. It's simply a matter of letting my mind attain a critical mass of table information. Without conscious self-instruction on my part (*That guy calls with bad kickers, so bet for value*) I'll come to a point where I play generally correctly against everyone. It's not magic and it is real. I've seen it happen time after time.

So now I go looking for it. I treat my first few laps around the table as a necessary evil, something I have to go through to get to the good part. I play these laps very snugly because I don't want to give away edge to foes I haven't figured out yet, and because I don't want to be in any kind of deep hole when the gestalt finally kicks in. It's not like I never play a hand, but I don't go looking for excuses to get involved, especially with reckless adventures. Nor do I feel like I'm depriving myself of either action or profit opportunities. Rather, by watching and waiting I'm investing in the gestalt, and I expect that investment to pay dividends later.

Does the gestalt always kick in? No, not always. Sometimes the players are coming and going so fast that I just don't have time to figure them all out. Sometimes, alas, my concentration isn't there. Instead of embracing the challenge of the clear gestalt, I let my mind wander . . . to the TV set or the cocktail waitress or the crossword puzzle. Sometimes it's hubris that blocks the clear gestalt: If I'm not careful, I can come to believe that this innate understanding is something that's mine by right, something I don't have to work at or earn.

You do have to work at it. You have to watch every hand, every bet, every set of eyes, every action. It's not particularly difficult work, just a matter of paying thoughtful attention to the game and the players. Relax. Be patient. Watch. Wait. Ghost your foes. Speculate on holdings. Stay engaged. Enjoy the challenge of absorbing the game from an observer's point of view. Eventually, everything will click into place and, like turning on a light, you'll acquire the clear gestalt.

For some players this will be impossible. It's not just because they're inattentive (they are) but because they block their own perceptions with impatience, anxiety, anger, ego, greed, fear, resentment, or other obfuscation. They may be so busy thinking, for example, *I'm not getting good cards and life is unfair* that they are literally unable to acquire and retain meaningful information.

Me, I'm in no hurry. Having experienced the clear gestalt, I'm willing to wait as long as I have to, not just for the cards to run good but for my mind to run good as well. Let's look at a graphic representation. There are four possible combinations of *cards* and *gestalt:*

bad cards	GOOD CARDS
no gestalt	*no gestalt*
bad cards	GOOD CARDS
CLEAR GESTALT	*CLEAR GESTALT*

I can't win with bad cards and no gestalt. I *might* win with good cards and no gestalt or with bad cards and clear gestalt, but if I wait until I have both good cards and clear gestalt, then I have everything going for me. I still might not win, for there's such a thing as bad luck, but by waiting for the optimum combination of cards and awareness, I'm giving myself every advantage when I play.

I still hate that first hand I play, but now I put it in perspective. It's the moment of maximum disadvantage, because I know nothing, but it's also the first step down the road toward moments of maximum advantage. If I can minimize the damage of the first hand, and the first few rounds of play, I can put myself in position to win when my mind finally gets hold of the game.

The next time you play hold'em, divide your session in two. Treat the first part of the session as the part where you *figure stuff out,* and the second part as the part where you *use what you know.* Finding the clear gestalt is like riding a bicycle: Once you learn, you'll never forget how.

SHORT-HANDED PLAY

Someone once asked me why hold'em tables are spread ten-handed in Las Vegas, but only nine-handed in California. Not having an immediate answer, I canvassed for opinions, and got some interesting ones. One compatriot noted that you can order food and eat meals at the table in California, but not in Las Vegas. With people leaving to eat, then, tables in Vegas run a greater risk of becoming short-handed or breaking altogether. For the sake of holding the game together, he speculated, they spread ten-handed as a form of insurance against takers of long breaks.

A second possible explanation lies in the fact that most Las Vegas cardrooms collect their money in the form of a percentage rake from the pot, while in Southern California it's either time collection or a straight drop from each hand. It is thus postulated that Vegas cardrooms stand to make more money by dealing to more players and creating the potential for larger pots, trending toward maximum rakes. Hmm . . . maybe.

For my money, the answer lies in the German word *Lebensraum,* or "living room." Poker rooms in Las Vegas are generally crowded into corners or otherwise consigned to limited space. Even the most expansive room constantly has to fend off encroachment from more lucrative per-square-foot money earners like slots and video poker machines. Space, in other words, is at a premium. In Southern California, poker shares no floor space with pull toys. If there's demand for a new game, a new game can be spread. It is this room to grow that mandates the custom of the California nine. Spreading nine-handed games assures that there will be more people waiting to play, more games being spread, and more drop being generated for the house.

Why do Southern California cardrooms spread nine-handed games? Answer: Because they can. They've got space to burn in the barn, and the reward of spreading extra games outweighs the risk of some games going short. This raises a question of no small interest: When does a game become too short-handed to be profitable?

Answer: When there's nobody left at the table.

Seriously, though, many hold'em players have strong aversions to the short-handed game, aversions worth examining and thinking about and, if necessary, overcoming.

Let's start by asking ourselves why a player might object to playing short-handed. Possible answers include:

- He doesn't think he's getting fair value vis-à-vis the rake.
- He has no effective strategy for short-handed play.
- He doesn't enjoy playing short-handed.
- He is *afraid.*

The first answer carries a little weight if the house's cut is taken in certain ways. If the game is short-handed but still fully raked, then fewer players will pay proportionally more of the rake per pot. If money is taken as a collection before the pot is even played (like they used to do in California), then each player at a short-handed table will pay more by paying more frequently. But if players are paying an hourly seat rental fee, then they'll actually get more bang for their buck by playing more hands per hour. Granted, those pots will be smaller, as a function of fewer players entering each pot, but also the competition will be reduced, so that should be about a wash.

Unless you don't know how to play short-handed, or unless you don't do it well, or unless you are afraid.

Many players just have a gut objection to playing short-handed. To them it doesn't seem to be like real hold'em, and they simply refuse to participate. This is something we have all seen: As soon as a couple of players wander away from the table, some crusty veteran will insist on sitting out until the table fills up once again. Despite entreaties—or even reductions in the house rake—this wily expert isn't going to put his money into play unless he has a full field of foes to play into.

Personally, I think this is misguided, short-sighted or, hey, let's not mince words, just plain wrong. Of this crafty old-timer, or of any active hold'em player, I would ask the question *What are you afraid of?* Do you imagine that the players arrayed against you in a short-handed game are somehow significantly better than you? If that's the case, weren't they better than you when the game was full? No? Did they somehow acquire mysterious super powers when the game went short? Or are you so unsure of your own hold'em skills in a short-handed game that you just feel like you're giving away too much equity to those more ex-perienced or capable in short-handed play? And if that's the case, why not just improve your short-handed game? Gain a little experience at short-handed play, and soon you can be one of those players whom other players want nothing to do with when the game goes short. All you have to do is know what to expect and how to adjust.

First, against fewer opponents you can expect to face fewer strong hands. Recall that in a ten-handed game, an average of two players will start with an ace or a pair. As the number of players drops, the average number of quality starts drops along with it. Bad aces go up in value because they're less likely to be up against good aces. Little pairs and un-paired big cards likewise go up in value because they stand a greater chance of winning without improvement. In a short-handed game, then, you should crank down your starting requirements.

At the same time, crank up your aggressiveness.

Short-handed play puts a premium on ferocity, which is one reason why the neenies and lemmies don't like it. They want to sit and wait, but they can't afford to. *You* can't af-ford to. You have to *attack*. Bring in more hands for a raise, and defend your good hands with reraises. Remember that your opponents are less likely to have quality cards and more likely, as you are, to recognize the need to step it up.

This propels everyone in the short-handed game into a sort of parallel hold'em universe where the normal rules and tactics don't apply.

Defense of blinds is of critical importance when playing short-handed, because the blinds come around so much more quickly. In a four-handed game, you're playing for a half or a full forced bet fully 50 percent of the time. If you either over-defend or under-defend your blinds, you'll start siphoning cash at a ferocious rate. Here we arrive at the real beauty of short-handed play: If your foes are prone to making bad decisions, you can put them to *many more decisions* than they'd otherwise face. Defense of blinds is a perfect example of this. Suppose you encounter a foe in a full-handed ring game who'll "take a flier" on his blind with just about any hand. T-8 offsuit, 9-3 suited, he doesn't care. He won't be bullied off his blind.

But he can be bullied off the flop.

You've figured this out, and you have responded accordingly, by raising his blind with almost anything, and by attacking any flop that looks the least bit scary. Your opponent routinely calls your raise preflop, then throws his hand away if and when he doesn't hit. This is a mistake, and a bad one, but in a full, ten-handed game, it's only happening on 10 percent of the hands he's dealt. A flaw, yes, but not a fatal one.

Now look at that same leak in a short-handed game. Instead of misplaying one hand out of ten, he's misplaying one hand out of four. The impact of that one error is amplified 2.5 times. And that's not counting how he plays the small blind!

Most players who defend their blinds too loosely or too passively also attack others' blinds too seldom, because they don't know how to be aggressive or can't bring themselves to bet with nothing. They have not awakened to the fact that their actual holdings now matter much less and their pattern of betting now matters much more.

As do their reads.

In a full ring game, you often don't need much special insight into how your opponents approach the game. If you're looking at a flop of K♥-T♥-3♣, and there's a bet and a raise and three calls before it gets to you, you don't need to know anything about the individual players to know that you're looking at big hands and big draws. But suppose you take that same flop heads up in a short-handed game and face a bet from your single opponent. You'd damn well like to know if he's a true value player, at least to the extent of having *some* of that flop, or if he, like you, knows that short-handed play puts a premium on aggressiveness, and he's trying to drive you off the pot with a naked ace or less. Likewise, you'd like to know how he'll respond to a reraise. Will he fold his tent, or will he figure that you're just as out-of-line frisky as he is?

The good news about short-handed play is you have fewer foes to figure out. The bad news is that the price for inattention is high. Here we see another reason why some players don't like short-handed play: They're lazy. They're used to, and happy with, hold'em situations that more or less play themselves. They don't want to work so hard at solving their opponents—or else it's an aptitude they lack and can't acquire.

I don't imagine that this is an aptitude *you* lack. You're used to paying attention in a poker game. You're used to playing appropriately, whether that means taking a free card when one is offered or driving a bare-ass bluff into a player who you know (from having watched) will not have the guts to call. Maybe you've shied away from short-handed hold'em up till now, for the simple reason that conventional wisdom seems to disdain the game. Screw conventional wisdom. Get in there and mix it up! Sure, there are adjust-ments to be made, but there's also money to be won. Sure, there are times you'd rather not be involved. Any time you know you're outclassed or outgunned by your foes, it's bet-ter not to play. Just don't get scared off by a few empty seats. You're a Killer Poker player; let *them* fear *you.*

To make them fear you all the more, throw a little game theory into the mix.

The easiest way to understand game theory, at least as it pertains to poker, is to look at what happens when you bluff. To make this discussion even easier, we'll invent a new version of poker, called "two-card poker." The two-card poker deck contains only two cards, the A♠ and the 2♣. You—and only you—are dealt one of the two cards, and now have the option of betting one chip or folding. If you bet, your opponent can either call or fold. If she calls, you show your card. With the ace, you win; with the deuce, you lose. On every deal, then, you're either going to win one chip, lose one chip, or have no action.

Now suppose you bet every time, whether you have the ace or not. Once your foe catches on, she'll call every time. There will be action on every hand, but since the proposi-tion is a straight 50/50, in the long run no one will make any money. Alternatively, what if you bet every ace and fold every deuce? Again, once your opponent gets wise to this, she'll never, ever call, because she'll know she can only lose. Either you won't bet or she won't call, and no money will change hands.

Are we having fun yet?

The real problem with either always betting or never betting is that it gives your opponent control over the out-come of the game. She can either choose to play or not to play, so that once you've acted, your fate is in her hands. Wouldn't it be better to put *her* fate in your hands? This you can do, according to game theory, by bluffing with correct frequency.

If your opponent thinks you bluff all the time, and thus calls every bet, you'll win only those outcomes in which you have an ace—exactly half, for zero profit. Likewise, if you bet an equal number of aces and deuces, you'll have an equal number of wins and losses against a foe who always calls. But what if you bet, say, every ace, but also half your deuces? Now you're betting two aces for every deuce. If your opponent continues to call every bet, you'll end up winning two-thirds of the time. Yes, your opponent will catch on, and yes, she'll try to adjust, but unless she calls with exactly the same frequency with which you bluff, she'll end up calling either too often or too rarely. And the beauty of game theory is *only you know how frequently you're bluffing.* Since your foe can't know, but only guess, she's bound to err on one side or the other. Now the decision is still in your opponent's hands, but you've arranged things in such a way that she can only make a perfect decision by luck or by somehow knowing the exact frequency with which you bluff.

If she calls too often, she pays you off when you have a winner. If she calls too rarely, she misses opportunities to catch you bluffing. She is at variance from optimum, and pretty much always will be, no matter what she does.

Now let's take the discussion back to short-handed hold'em, and the business of attacking the blinds. If your opponent in the big blind is aware of game theory, she's looking for the correct calling frequency. She knows you can't have the goods all the time, but she doesn't know when you do and when you don't. Can you use game theory to put her in a situation where she might make mistakes? Yup. Sure can.

First, imagine what happens if you raise with good cards

and bad cards alike. Your opponent soon figures out that you don't always have the goods, and increases her calling frequency. On the other hand, if you only raise with good cards, your opponent will call less often, and minimize her loss. To use game theory to your advantage, simply raise with *all* of your good hands and *some arbitrary number* of your stiffs. Your foe ends up playing too tight or too loose unless (by pure luck) she finds the right calling frequency.

How many of your stiffs should you play? The answer is . . . some. You could, for example, choose to raise every time you hold two black unsuited or two red unsuited cards lower than eight. Though we could do the math to figure out the exact frequency with which you would now be bluff-raising into your foe's blind, in fact it really doesn't matter. Your frequency is arbitrary and unknowable, and your opponent must naturally end up on one side of correct or the other.

In poker this is called *mixing up your play*, and *putting your opponent to a hard choice*. Game theory reduces this concept to a mathematical certainty. Bluff with a certain frequency: more than never, less than always. If you do this, it doesn't matter whether you win or lose on an individual hand. You've put your opponent to a hard choice—not just a hard choice, but an impossible one! No matter what she does, she can't make the right decision all the time.

Then again, it's best not to get too carried away with this stuff. Your opponents are not automatons, and they're not completely ignorant. They're constantly looking for tells, and they may be better at picking them off than you give them credit for. At the same time, you're collecting evidence, too. Without very much study, you can classify most opponents as *too loose* or *too tight*. Bluff less frequently against the former and more frequently against the latter, and let game theory go chase its own tail.

In any case, real success in short-handed play comes not so much from extracting the odd extra bet here and there, but from taking over the table. Game theory and bluffing frequency aside, if you can get your (few) opponents consistently leaning the wrong way against you, you can beat them like red-headed stepchildren. Mix up your play completely. Slow-play sometimes. Push middle suited connectors like they're pocket aces. Put your opponents on the wobble. Force them to make *so many* decisions against *so unpredictable* a foe that they almost can't help but get it wrong. More than anything else, keep the pressure on. If you're up against foes who feel at all uncomfortable playing short-handed, simply turn up the heat and make them more uncomfortable still. Their own discomfort will soon become a negative factor in their play. Hold'em in general rewards being the bus driver; short-handed success pretty much totally demands it.

WHAT ARE YOU LOOKING AT?

I want you to make a change in your table behavior. It'll take some getting used to, but once you acquire the habit, it will become second nature. Are you ready? Okay, here it comes.

> Never watch the flop again.

Never watch another flop. Or a turn, or a river, for that matter. Never see a card fall. Instead, every time the dealer burns and turns, make sure that you're watching someone else who *is* watching the reveal. There are several good reasons for this. Can you think of them?

I can think of three. Two will be obvious, but one might take you by surprise.

1. They might give something away. If you're in the right kind of game—a game, that is, with at least some weak and exploitable players—you can pick off direct tells by watching those who watch the flop. Sometimes it's nothing more than a cheek-twitch. Sometimes you see an actual flinch, or a sag of disappointment: *That wasn't what I wanted!* Other times, you'll see someone's eyes darting around the table, on the hunt for other interested parties. This is someone who plans to be involved. Occasionally you'll see the eyes move from the board . . . to the TV screen! A sure sign that the player has lost interest in the flop.

Or is it? Is it not true that some players will feign disinterest in a flop or a turn or a river card that they're truly very happy with? Of course it's true. Tricky players, those in control of their gestures as well as their emotions, can give off all sorts of false information. But don't you already know who they are? Haven't you already cataloged the players at your table and divided them into *tricky* and *straightforward* categories? If you have, it is then a simple matter to correlate their responses with their true feelings. Straightforward players tell it like it is. If they're not careful, they tell it very expressively. But they only tell it briefly, which is why you should be watching *them,* not the cards, when the cards hit the felt.

2. If you don't watch the cards fall, you can't give off a tell. In a perfect world, you're the only Killer Poker player at the table at any given time. Ours, alas, is not a perfect world, and some of your foes are at least as observant and diligent as you are. They're not watching the flop. They're watching you watching the flop. They're hoping you'll essay a twitch or a smile or a frown or a sniff or something that tells them how you feel about the cards you've just seen. If nothing else, they're looking to see what you're looking at. If your eyes are on the board, they know you're not as attentive as you should be, and they can attack you accordingly. If, on the other hand, they glance at you and *see you glancing at them,* they'll know they're in the presence of a cagey foe. That's good. If they respect you or fear you, they won't be so tempted to make plays at you. Remember, half the battle in any hold'em game is exploiting weak foes, but the other half is blunting the attacks of tough ones. When your eyes meet—when you catch one another not looking at the flop—your glance sends a message: *I'm on to you.*

You learned long ago not to look at your hole cards until it was your turn to act. You've known all along that savvy opponents were watching when you peeked, trying to gauge your level of enthusiasm. By not looking until after they acted, you quickly realized, you couldn't give anything away. The same logic applies to not watching the cards fall. If they never catch you looking, they'll never catch a tell.

3. You plan more moves in advance. Knowing that you're not going watch a flop, turn, or river, you find yourself anticipating the various cards you might see. If you're holding K-Q, for example, you're looking for a flop that contains a king or a queen, but doesn't contain an ace. Suppose you're the second of several to act. You're watching the player in front of you watch the flop. Even before he checks, you know by his body language that he's lost all interest. Now you let your eyes graze quickly across the flop. You don't have to decide what to do with it—just decide which of your previously constructed subroutines to run. You've already anticipated this situation: *King or queen, no ace, I bet; any ace, I check.* Your actions are as fluid and natural as if you'd been staring hard at the cards. Plus, you know at least one player who no longer cares to contend.

I hope you can see the benefit of this. You become proactive instead of reactive. You start running scripts instead of making unplanned plays. You integrate your individual actions into your overall game strategy. You avoid impulsive acts. You are now literally a step ahead of the competition. All because you stopped doing what everyone else does: paying slavish attention to the reveal.

Never see the cards fall again. It's a missed opportunity at best and a terrible tell at worst.

Now, as I said, this is a habit that takes some time and effort to acquire. The siren's song of the flop is so strong that it's often difficult to tear your eyes away. After all, the unknown is about to become known. You're only human. You want that information. It's important information, and you don't want to wait to get it. All your further actions in the hand depend on the turn of cards. No wonder you're so fixated.

But what about hands you're not in? You don't care about those flops and turns and rivers, do you? Can you see, then, what a marvelous opportunity you have not just for training yourself off flop-watching but also for delving deep into your foes' souls? Much is revealed when the cards are revealed. When you're out of the hand, make it your practice always to be watching somebody. Maybe they'll give nothing away—okay, then you know they're capable of protecting themselves from their own reactions. Maybe they'll give much away—information you can use against them in subsequent hands. In any case, you'll be astounded to see how few of your foes ever do anything but stare at the board.

> *Tommy Tomato looks at the flop, and disdain paints his face. He check-calls the flop, check-raises the turn, and at the showdown reveals that he'd flopped top set. You weren't in the hand, but the hand was probably more valuable to you than it was to Tommy, for now you know how Tommy handles top flops. He feigns disdain, tries to trap. Next time you're up against him and you see him give that look, you'll know not to fall into his trap. All because you paid attention to his face when you weren't involved in a hand.*

> *Is Tommy on to you? Of course he's not on to you. He never took his eyes off the cards.*

What sort of players should you watch when you're not involved? I have several that I'm interested in.

Those with tells. If I've discovered players who routinely give information away, I'll study them hard and build up, if you will, a vocabulary of flop-tells. Nor are their tells limited to their eyes. Watch the hands. An involuntary move toward a player's chips or his cards can tell you whether he plans to call or muck.

The last raiser. It's always useful to see how the person driving the action feels about the next card. Especially in games where check-raises are prevalent, you'd like to know whether a check is really a check. A raiser's unguarded reaction to the fall of a card may tell you what you need to know.

Strong players. Tough players are your biggest challenge, and they're worthy of your best attention. At first they may seem to give nothing away, but over time you become attuned to even the subtlest clues. You may not even be consciously aware of your read. You may just start to get a sense of whether they're genuinely happy or sad, checked in or checked out. This information contributes directly to your clear gestalt, but it's only available to you if you go get it.

So go get it. Next time you go play poker, write yourself a little note that asks,

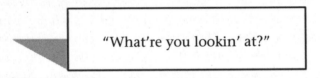

"What're you lookin' at?"

Put it on the table where you can see it. Try to convince yourself that watching the cards hit the felt is somehow taboo. Over time it will become so, and you'll find yourself routinely looking at the other players, where the truly useful information lies.

WELL, THAT HAPPENS

It's a well-known fact of hold'em life that good players get sucked out on more often than bad players, simply because good players put themselves in situations of negative expectation much less often than the bad ones do. Nevertheless, it takes a certain amount of fortitude (above and beyond the secret knowledge/hope/faith that the suckout artists will get what they deserve in time) to deal with a circumstance like this.

You find yourself in the big blind with pocket kings. Because it's *that kind* of game, there's a raise under the gun and six—count 'em, six!—callers before it gets back around to you. Much as you like pocket kings in general, you don't like them all that much here because you know you're an underdog to this crowded field. How big a dog? Pocket kings will win more often than any of seven other random hands, but it will still lose to the field about two-thirds of the time. The first choice you face is whether to three-bet this pot. If you just call, you hide the strength of your hand. But raising seems like a better idea, because those who fold will narrow the field, which you want, and those who call are, individually at least, calling with the worst of it. Not that you expect anyone to fold, and no one defeats that expectation when you raise. No one caps it either, so you figure that you're up against the usual assortment of weak aces, stupid connectors, and muddling pairs. Perilous! With so many callers, most flops will give somebody something and few flops will tell you clearly where you're at. You can dream of K-6-6 (and trust that nobody flopped quads) or K-7-4 (and hope that nobody's married to a 5-6 that gets there) or even A-x-x (which will at least let you get away from your hand).

The flop comes 8♥-7♣-2♥. Great. Now all you have to fear is a set, two pairs, a straight draw, or a flush draw. The pot is so big that anyone with anything is strapped in for the river run. Forget about being drawn out on—against this wacky field, you're not at all sure you even have the best hand now. You're not convinced that any turn card but a king is safe. You might like a deuce to give you top and bottom pair, but what about a suited A-2 that called preflop? Now he's got trips and you're drawing dead to a king.

So you check. The player to your immediate left bets out, and you feel that this pretty well defines his hand as top pair, top kicker, or else an overpair to the board. You wonder if it might be aces, though, and when four calls and two folds bring the action back around to you, you decide to find out. You fire off a check-raise. The original raiser just calls, so you now figure that he doesn't have aces. One of the original downstream callers surprises you by folding. You guess that he didn't have a draw, but rather a lonesome pair that he decided not to get too loopy over after all. The other three players call. They all watch the turn card come, but you watch the original bettor, trying to glean a tell. He doesn't seem all that happy with an offsuit queen, so you now put him on pocket jacks or tens.

What about the other callers? What are they on (besides pain medication)? Straight draws or flush draws, you assume, for if someone had had two pair or a set, you'd probably have heard about it either before or after your check-raise on the flop. Tenuous as your holding has felt up till this point, it's starting to look like the best hand, and now seems like no time to be handing out gift cards, so you bet. The original raiser drops out, meaning that your read on him was right. The three remaining foes all call. No one looks happy, but no one is going away either. All eyes (except yours) are on the river card as it falls. . . .

. . . *In a parallel universe, the river is an offsuit king. You bet, they call, and you rake a monster pot. . . .*

Hah! Sorry, this isn't a parallel universe. This is this universe, and the river card is an ace, suited to the board. You wonder if you have a bet here. Can you make all three foes believe that you'd been driving a flush draw all the way from your preflop three-bet? And even if you can make them believe, *can you make them fold?* There's just a buttload of bets in the pot right now (20.5 big bets, to be precise). Even if no one's on the flush (which they may very well be), anyone with an ace will certainly call you down. If you thought your kings were good, you could bet for value, but you don't rate that as a reasonable expectation, so you check.

And they all check, too. You allow yourself a moment's hope that, incredibly, your kings have held up (against what? 9-8? T-9? 7-7?) but two—count 'em, two!—of your remaining foes turn over A-3 to split the giganzo pot. More than $400 in a $10–$20 game! (More than $4.00 in a 1¢–2¢ game!)

All theirs.

None yours.

Darkness falls.

There were different ways to play this hand. You could have not raised preflop, or led the betting on the flop, or gone for a check-raise on the turn. None of these alternatives would have changed the outcome, however. In a game filled with cally wallies (the exact sort of game you love to be in) you got sucked out on. Now you have to deal with that.

Do this: Mentally puff out your cheeks and say to yourself, "Well, that happens." Don't call yourself unlucky. Don't hate the pumpkins with the A-3s for making promiscuous bad calls—how can you hate a player who makes promiscuous bad calls? Especially don't cry out loud about your skewered paired paint. What would be the point? You'd just reinforce the notion that you're an unlucky loser. If you must say anything, say this:

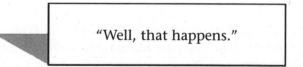

"Well, that happens."

I've described this hand in some detail because it demonstrates the two separate but equally important parts to our thinking about hold'em hands. The first part is the play of the hand itself, and the second part is the reaction to the outcome. As we've seen, there's more than one way to play this hand correctly. But there's only one way to deal with the outcome correctly.

With equanimity.

Take it in stride.

Handling the beat is no less important than playing the hand correctly. It's more important, in fact, because if you screw up the play of the hand it only costs you that hand, but if you screw up your reaction to the beat it will continue to cost you for many hands to come. You already know this. You already know how bad beats can trigger tilt. But this isn't garden-variety tilt we're talking about here. This is an infection that, if left unchecked, will sink to the core of our being, spread throughout our perception, alter the way we see the game from this point forward, and utterly destroy our play. To check the infection, to stop its spread, just inoculate yourself with three little words, *Well, that happens.* Apply the medicine immediately and repeat as necessary. Treat the wound, then treat the past as passed. Above all, appreciate the distinction between review and regret. To improve your play, review your play. Figure out what you might have done wrong or could have done better. Spend no time regretting the outcome. You can change the way you play, but you can't change an outcome. Especially not one in the past.

Well, that happens.

A pumpkin defends his blind with 9-2 offsuit. (Why didn't he fold?!) He flops two pair and takes you off for many bets. Well, that happens.

A dealer deals you pocket aces, but, oops, forgets to deal another player in. It's a misdeal, and the cards go back, including your precious pocket aces. Well, that happens.

A maniac reraises your legitimate hand with absolute gravel. You know he's way out of line and happily go to war. He draws to a four-outer (or a two-outer) (or a one-outer!) and gets there. Well, that happens.

In this hold'em universe of ours there's no shortage of bad players and no shortage of adverse outcomes. Can you think of certain circumstances that have irked you or pained you or made you feel, to quote Paul Simon, "sat upon, spat upon, ratted on"? Please list them here.

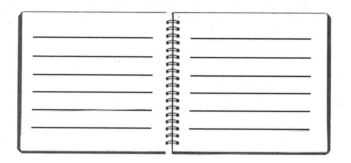

Now re-read your list, and remind yourself, "Well, that happens." Let it be your mantra. Remember, the universe doesn't owe you anything except an education. You may feel like you're getting more than your fair share of lessons, but each setback is an opportunity to flex your "well, that happens" muscle. It's a muscle worth building.

And if in the moment of torment you still can't set aside your pain, remember why you joined this particular game in the first place: *because it was a good game.* Because it featured a high percentage of loose, passive, undereducated neenies who don't know enough to fold with the worst of it. Because the raw math of hold'em says that selective-aggressive play must, in the long run, win more money than sucking out. Because bad players are your bread and butter, but if they never beat the odds, they'd never play the game, and then where would we be? Without bread. Without butter.

Well, that happens.

There are two sides to every drawing situation. If you're on a crazy draw, like a two-outer with one card to come, you'll get there around 4 percent of the time. If you're on the other side of the draw, defending against it, you'll win that battle more than *nine times out of ten!* Confirmation bias makes it seem like we're *always* getting sucked out on, but we tend to forget all those uneventful hands where we drive a quality holding into a draw that doesn't get there, and rake the pot without a second thought. Confirmation bias makes us bemoan the suckouts and forget all the times the suckouts don't happen. Look, a good game is a good game is a good game. You may not beat it on this very hand, but you will beat it in the long run. That's the very definition of a good game: one you can beat in the long run.

If the short run daunts you and taunts you and tears you still, just learn to say, "Well, that happens." Even if you don't believe it, saying it will make you seem tranquil in the face of the bad beat, and the *appearance* of tranquility puts you halfway on the road to the *fact* of tranquility. As the saying goes, "Fake it till you make it." Pretend that the suckout didn't hurt, and keep pretending until the pain of the suckout fades away.

Another hand is being dealt right now. It's not important that you win the hand. It is important that you play it right.

5

♣ ♠ ♦ ♥

HARD-CORE HOLD'EM

♧ ♤ ◇ ♡

In this section we'll take a more detailed look at some hold'em moments and hold'em choices. Please remember that there are no guaranteed solutions to most hold'em problems, and that it can be rash or foolish to blindly apply a given set of strategies or tactics to your game. The subtle read you have on a certain player, the texture of the table, the state of your image, the betting limits, or other variables can often make the difference between a workable stratagem and a disaster. I'm not saying that you should take the following advice with a grain of salt; I'm recommending, rather, that you season to taste.

TRUE OR FALSE

As you consider the following postulates, take a moment to contemplate whether you think they're true or false, and why. Bearing in mind that "the ocean is blue, but it's also wet," remember that there's often more than one right answer.

True or False: House players are less likely to be out of line when they attack the blinds.

True. House players—shills and props—are in it for the long haul. They profit in the long run by playing true value poker, not by squeezing out a little extra equity from marginal situations. Because they have a need for a low-variance, steady profit situation, they have less incentive to get frisky than the recreational player (or certainly the compulsive gambler) does. Those who get too frisky too frequently go broke and remove themselves from the house player pool, in the very same way that unfavorable mutations select themselves out of a species' gene pool.

When you're in a game with house players (assuming you've made the effort to discover who they are) be less inclined to defend your blind against them without a hand of some kind. On the other hand, if you suspect that the house player (or any other true value player) will only raise your blind with wheelhouse cards and up, you can put him on a narrow range of hands and attempt to steal the pot if the flop comes antagonistic to high cards.

House players have one of the hardest easy jobs in the world. Yes, they're being paid to play poker, and doesn't that seem like funded fun? But they're the first players into a bad game and the first players out of a good one. They lose a fundamental freedom of poker: the freedom to choose their game. Those who overcome this handicap have the temperament of a Trappist monk and a shell of pure plastron. Over time—whether they know it or not—they become accustomed to playing a very cagey, very defensive brand of hold'em. They have no need for reckless adventures such as bluffing or driving or promiscuously attacking blinds, even with a high probability of success. I do not disparage them by calling them *grinders*, for grinding, in their case, is a strategy that works.

But it does make them timid, after a fashion. Not timid like a weak player is timid, just cautious; reluctant to mix it up. For example, just as they're less likely to attack blinds without a real hand, they're also less likely to defend their blinds without some plausible ammunition. Remember, they're thinking long term. They realize that over-defense of blinds is a hole in most players' games—a hole they can't afford to fall into. They'd rather sacrifice that one small bet than risk getting involved in a shooting war where they're out of position and can't control the hand. Their profit comes from preying on the weak, not defending against the strong. *Be* strong against these players. If you train them (through aggressiveness) not to tangle with you, you'll find that you can attack their blinds with reasonable impunity.

True or False: Losing is part of winning.

Absolutely true. Some might be inclined to say "sadly true," but I think they're misguided in attaching sadness to losing. Losing isn't bad, nor is it good. It has no value until we assign it value, and if we assign it a negative value, it can only bring us down. This doesn't mean that we should grow complacent or tolerant of losing. No Killer Poker player *wants* to lose. But no sensible and self-aware poker player clings to the fantasy of winning all the time. It just doesn't happen, and if we think that it will happen, we're setting ourselves up for disappointment.

Poker is a challenge. Maybe you wish it weren't. Maybe you wish you could walk into the casino or cardroom, put in your hours, and walk away with an exact, guaranteed return for your time. Yes? Then why aren't you working at Starbucks? They'll give you an exact, guaranteed return for your time. It may not be enough money for you, and you may not enjoy it, but it will certainly be a sure thing. If working at Starbucks doesn't float your boat like playing poker does, then it's time to admit that challenge is why you're there. And the possibility of failure is implied in challenge. If there were no possibility of failure, there would simply be no challenge. To put it another way, if you hit the target every time, the target is either too big or too close—and it's no fun either way.

There's no sure thing in hold'em. This we know. Yet we get all weepy and sad when we lose. The way I see it, the problem is not the losing, the problem is all the weepy sadness that follows in its wake. If we can just disconnect from that negative emotion, then we can sally forth the next time with a light heart, a clear mind, and a pack of winning tactics.

But disconnecting from emotion is a tricky business. Do too good a job and you won't *care* if you lose. If you don't care at all about the outcomes, you may not invest sufficient energy to earn the positive outcomes you crave. So then we arrive at the following conundrum: *How can I detach from the pain of losing without detaching from the desire to win?*

The answer lies in a simple semantic shift: Change the word *win* to the word *excel*. A strong desire to win leaves you open to crushing disappointment when you lose, but a strong desire to *excel* will keep you passionately committed to playing your best all the time. Not only that, a strong desire to excel will actually help buttress your psyche against the pain of losing. It's a lot easier to deal with bad beats when they happen in the context of good play. Bad beats plus bad play equals despair. Bad beats plus good play? We can cope. We can take solace in knowing that, bad-beaten though we may have been, at least we played the damn hand right.

If this still seems too vague and airy-fairy for you, set some tangible targets. Tell yourself that in your next poker session, you will try to achieve one of these goals.

Run a board-driven bluff. *Look for a situation where any one of a number of scare-cards could hit the board on the turn or the river, and then own that card when it comes.*

Pick off a tell. *Invest some energy and some focus in really watching the other folks play and pick up some information you know to be 100 percent accurate.*

Work your image. *Project an image, any image. Make the effort to make your foes see you in a certain light and play against you not as you are, but as you seem to be.*

What other targets might you try to hit?

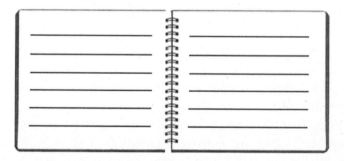

Losing is part of winning, but there are other parts of winning, too. See beyond the bottom line. If you focus on your achievements and the honing of your skills, the jellyfish-sting of losing tends to hurt a whole lot less.

True or False: When you've been caught out of line, that's the time to turn up the heat.

Exactly false. When you've been caught out of line, that's the time to go back to sleep. Gear your game down to its tightest and most straightforward. People tend to remember when you get out of line. They tend to treat you not as you generally are, but as you most recently were.

Say you drove a naked bluff all the way through the hand, and unfortunately some neeny called you down. Not only did you lose the pot, you lost a big chunk of image. Now you're suddenly *that guy who got caught bluffing,* and it's a label that will stay with you until you remove it by showing down a legitimate hand. Having been caught out of line, you have no choice but to put the bluff in your back pocket and wait for better cards or better times. (Actually, you do have other choices. You could change tables or games or clubs or even, in extreme cases, cities. Sometimes the best way to undo the damage of a broken image is just to take it someplace where it's not known to be broken.)

It's not the end of the world to be caught out of line. After all, if they think you're frisky and bluffy, they'll call you more often than they should. It is necessary, though, that you know where your image stands. Know, and be honest about whether you can expect to get called down or not. If you know they're going to call, then driving a bluff is not just silly, it's suicide.

Why would you do it? Why would you try to drive another bluff after just getting one snapped off? Could it be that the image you're concerned about is not *their* picture of you but *your* picture of you? For many players, it's humiliating to get caught bluffing. Even absent this emotional collateral damage, there is the fact that, well, you didn't win the pot. You may be trying to get well quick. You may be trying to repair your stack and your self-image simultaneously. This need to get well may very well overwhelm your normal cautious considerations. You know you got caught and you know you'll get caught again; yet you try just the same because you've got to take the curse off as quickly as possible.

How about this: Consider it a blessing, not a curse. No matter how shattered your image may be, it presents the opportunity to get others to play into it. Yes, you may have to wait for strong cards, but once you get them, and once you drive them home, you'll get paid off—two ways. First, you'll win extra bets that you wouldn't have won if they hadn't thought you bluffy. Second, your image will now flip from Bluffy the Vampire Player to Mr. True Value Hardware Store. And you will do everything in your power to reinforce this flip by making sure that everyone knows you know you got caught bluffing and resolved to play only solid cards.

This is the "light switch theory of image management." A garden variety light switch has only two states: on and off. Likewise, garden variety players can only hold one image of you in their minds: They see you as either plain or fancy. *But their opinion changes back and forth like a light turning off and on.* Get caught bluffing and you look tricky. Show down a powerhouse and you seem straightforward. Whatever image the table has of you, you have an immediate opportunity to act in an opposite fashion. When you've just shown down winners, your speculative hands can be bluffed more freely. When you've just been caught out of line, your solid hands can get paid off more liberally.

Some players can't master this trick, and you should be aware of who they are. If they get caught out of line, *they go right out again,* for the exact reason of psychic damage control outlined above. They simply can't stand the pain, and they're looking for immediate relief. Penalize them for feeling, rather than thinking, their game.

As for you, remember that everyone gets out of line from time to time. The best players know that they're doing it, know *why* they're doing it, and accept the outcomes that follow. The worst players don't even know they're out of line—or won't admit they're out of line—and punish themselves accordingly, both psychologically and financially, when they get caught.

True or False: Most preflop raises look like a big ace to most players.

Well, I haven't done a survey, and even if I had done a survey I'm not sure I could trust the results since, shockingly, some players lie, but I do think it's true that most players' first reaction to a preflop raise is to put the raiser on ace-big. Why? Well, most raises *are* ace-big. Thanks to the profusion of hold'em books, simulations, discussion groups, and start charts, most players consider an A-K raise to be automatic, a no-brainer. Since hold'em is a slippery slope, many players extend their enthusiasm for the A-K down to A-Q, A-J, A-T. They may even get moist over A-9 if it's suited. In any case, this promiscuous raising with aces has created a certain group mentality about preflop raising: *Sure, he* might *have a big pair, but since ace-big comes around so much more frequently than the big pairs, that's probably the hand he has.*

Curiously, in some loose and weak hold'em circles (the kind of circles we like to run around in) the fear of an ace from the raiser won't dissuade the wallies from calling. They'll jump in with their K-8 suiteds and other gork, clinging with the faith of true believers to the notion that an ace can't flop *all* the time. They're right about this; assuming that there's one ace out there in somebody's hand, an ace will hit the flop about 18 percent of the time. Still, they fear the ace because they believe it hits the raiser's hand. If you're fortunate enough to play against foes who fall into this *raise = ace* trap, it creates a marvelous and consistent steal opportunity for you. Go ahead and raise with almost any semi-solid holding (for example, K-Q or middle pocket pairs) and seek to isolate against those who will call with less than aces. Mostly these are hit-to-win types who are looking for non-ace flops they can use to snap off the ace-big hand they assume you have.

By raising with non-ace hands into players who put you on ace hands, you give yourself additional outs. Not only might you yourself hit-to-win, you could also flop an ace, and this is a circumstance you have already predetermined to own. (Note that your not having an ace increases the chance of an ace hitting the board. With no aces spoken for, an ace will flop around 25 percent of the time.) The ace hits, you bet, your foe bemoans his rotten luck and folds.

If your image is right you can make this move regardless of the cards you hold. But you won't, because you know that the ace you're looking for will only come one time out of four or less. What makes this play profitable is the sum of your outs, ace and non-ace alike. If the flop doesn't come with an ace, as it most often won't, mostly you're going to have to dump your hand—unless you have those additional outs. Save this play for times when you hold a couple of wheelhouse cards, and you'll increase your odds of hitting a little somethin'-somethin' on the flop, even if you don't hit the magic bullet you're looking for.

A caveat: This play runs into danger in the very type of game where it's most likely to be successful. You're looking to make this raise into a field of weak, loose foes, but these foes, almost by definition, fall below the anyace line, and will call with bad aces in addition to that other slag. And you know it's true that players capable of calling a raise with A-6 offsuit are not likely to let the fear of a better ace drive them off their hands when the flop comes A-9-3. They're bluff-proof, whether they put the raiser on an ace or not. Go ahead and represent that phantom ace if you're so inclined, but be prepared to shut it down if they seem too eager to call.

Two underlying principles guide your action here.

First, see the table as it is. If your foes truly are bluff-proof, you'll gain nothing by trying to prove them otherwise. See them as they are, not as you wish them to be, and plan your moves accordingly. In any case, *plan your moves,* for hold'em becomes both more rewarding and more profitable when you're enacting situations and not just reacting to cards.

Second, see yourself as the table sees you. Know whether your enemies assume and fear the ace-big raise, and whether they see you as the guy who makes that raise. You can help convince them of this by showing a couple of ace-big laydowns, or doing a folding foe the "favor" of showing him you had him beat, for if you had the ace this time, he'll assume you have it next time, too. Once you're confident that the table views you as the "man with the plan for aces," you can go ahead and execute that plan—whether you hold the aces or not.

True or False: If they'll call for one, they'll call for two.

Generally true, because most players are consistent—and the bad ones are consistently bad. Weak, loose players make two related mistakes: They call with inferior values and they call instead of raise. This *errata perfecta* leaves them vulnerable to the downstream raise, and when faced with such a raise, the very mentality that led them to their first loose call now leads to a second. This is not just a case of throwing good money after bad. They may actually think that, having thrown a first bet into what is now becoming a sizeable pot, they have correct odds to call a raise. Or they may just want the action and not give a big fig about odds. Either way, with most loose, weak players, "If they're good for one, they're good for two."

So let's give 'em two, right? If they made the mistake of

calling in the first place, let's give 'em the chance to err again on the side of recklessness, right?

Right . . . within limits. If a large number of players have already entered the fray, and if this two-for-the-price-of-one mentality genuinely pervades, you cannot generally raise to isolate. It just won't work. You probably won't even drop the blinds, who figure that any halfway decent holding is getting implied odds from all the in-for-a-penny-in-for-a-pound-ers downstream. At that point, your raise will only succeed in building pot volume, and you should only make the raise with that goal in mind. While it's true that your foes (if they're the right foes) are mistake-prone drones, when there are a lot of them, even the best hands are underdogs to a large field taken as a whole.

So then what sort of hands do you want to raise with here? Top pairs and top draws. With so much traffic in the hand, you're going to need to hit to win, and you're going to need to overcome a large field to do it. You'd like to be drawing to a nut flush or nut straight, or—happy happenstance—riding top set. Note that a hand like J-J is not a raising hand in this case. It's just too vulnerable to an overcard flop. It plays more like a middle pair, looking for a cheap price and a volume pot—exactly what it will get if you don't raise here. Note also that some of your junk raisers like middle suited connectors are not at all playable here. Where you might hope to take 9-8 suited one-on-one against anybody, you don't have that possibility now. You can't even call with that hand, for if you did, you'd have to hit the flop twice in order to feel at all confident, and even then a flop like 9-8-7 will leave you with very little room to move. You'd have to bet to protect your shaky two pair and hope (probably in vain) that no one in a crowded field will cling to a naked 10 or 6, or a forlorn 7 in search of an ace. Best just to dump it and wait for better days.

> Curiously, hold'em is one game
> where you can often do better by
> doing nothing at all.

Call-and-call-again types are often dazzled by the beguiling prospect of pot odds. They reason that if the pot is big enough, or likely to grow big enough, they're justified in calling along with anything at all. They're often right, in the sense that the pot is theoretically offering the correct price for their call. What they forget, though, is that the pot is offering the same price to everyone. While their J♠-9♠ might be worth playing "for the size of the pot," so is K♠-2♠, and when that spade flush gets there, J♠-9♠ is going to be mighty unhappy, even though he had "odds" all along.

Don't fall into this trap. Even though the pot seems attractively large, bad hands remain bad hands. Maintain your starting requirements. You might be tempted to punish promiscuous callers by raising, but save your punishment raise for when your own hand is dominant. Remember the old good advice about playing tight in a loose game, for in a loose game you have to hit to win, and that's easier to do when you start with superior cards.

True or False: 9-8 can be a better hand to raise with than J-T.

I expect I'll take some heat for saying so, but in many situations I'd much rather raise with 9-8 than with J-T. It's a junk raise. I know it's a junk raise. But it's a junk raise with a purpose . . . a purpose that J-T can't achieve. If I find myself up against the typical wheelhouse crowd, I'll raise with 9-8 in hopes of hitting a flop I can drive, one bunched around my middle cards and without scary overcards. You get these flops from time to time: You hit top pair with a straight draw, drive the hand home and happily show down the cheese with which you raised. You'll win the pot and win some image points as well.

If you try the same trick with J-T, though, there's almost no flop you can like. Any jack or ten that flops will leave you vulnerable to the wheelhouse holdings of J-Q, J-K, A-T, etc. Likewise, a top pair/straight draw flop, of J-9-8 for example, risks running into either a made hand or a better draw. A must to avoid, then (if you're going to make junk raises), is a flop that connects to your hand, but connects better to someone else's. A genuine junk raise is designed to solidly hit your hand while solidly missing the wheelhouse hands.

What are my junk raise hands? 9-8, 8-7 and middle pairs. I don't go lower because I don't want to leave too much headroom above my holding, and I only make junk raises when there's a reasonable chance of isolating against predictable big-card players. I'm looking for a flop that comes middle-middle-middle or middle-middle-little. If I have any piece of that flop, I'm in the driver's seat. I want calls from overcards here (and I'll get 'em, 'cause people know I play junk). Even an A-K is drawing to only six outs, a 3-1 dog to get there between the flop and the river. With a small enough pot and a thin enough field, he's probably drawing with the worst of it.

I'll play middle pairs to a different end here. In a crowded house, I limp with middle pairs, looking for the volume I need to draw to a set. When my foes are few in number, and especially if they're weak, timid, or straightforward, I'm raising with middle pairs and looking for an overcard-free flop. If I raise with 7-7 and flop something like 8-6-4, my 7s are probably the best hand and I can continue with my junk raise strategy. Do I fear A-8? No. If I feel that my foes are capable of calling with A-8, I'm not making the junk raise in the first place.

You may sense an inherent conflict here. How can my foes be loose enough to chase with overcards, yet tight enough to fold A-8? I grant that there seems to be a contradiction—but perhaps my foes aren't loose enough to call with just overcards. Maybe they'll fold and I'll win the pot on the flop. In all events, there's no doubt that the junk raise is a delicate tool you can only use when the situation is exactly right. But don't forget its secondary benefit: If you raise with junk, and hit your junk, you'll get paid off for the rest of the session when you raise with quality hands. Above all, don't confuse semi-junk like J-T with real junk like 8-7. For this ploy to work, you must have a flop that hits you hard and totally misses everybody else. Also, don't confuse a junk raise with a junk call. The junk raise is a *purpose* raise, designed to win a pot under special circumstances and to send a misleading image message. A junk call is just a loose call, and that's a long-run loser.

True or False: When two games are spread at the same limit, the main game is generally tougher than the must-move game.

True . . . I think. Let's investigate.

We'll start—and I know it's gonna sound strange—by discussing the Brazil Nut Effect. This notion of physical motion predicts that when a vessel containing different sized objects (like a jar of mixed nuts, say) is shaken, the smaller objects migrate to the bottom and the larger objects migrate to the top. Why this happens has to do with such multisyllabic obscurities as intruder motion, fluidization, vibration-induced convection and interstitial air drag, but the simple explanation is that smaller objects can fall through smaller spaces, the better to obey gravity's relentless tug. This, any fan of sugar-coated peanuts will tell you, is why you open the Cracker Jack box upside down.

But what has it to do with main games and must-moves? Metaphorically, everything.

Imagine a universe of, say, $15–$30 hold'em players. Now divide that universe into stronger or weaker players— larger or smaller nuts, so to speak, in terms of ability or skills—and visualize them in a club where there's a $15–$30 must-move game and a main game. All players start out in the must-move game, rotating into the main game as seats become available. However, some of them don't last that long. The weakest, worst, tiltiest players actually bust out and quit before they're even summoned to the main game. So we already see a natural culling of (in)ability. Every player who makes it to the main game has demonstrated the ability to last at least long enough to do so.

The same dynamic is repeated in the main game. The best players win and stay; the worst players lose and leave. This trend may be reversed by short-term fluctuation (luck), just as the odd Brazil nut may find its way to the bottom of the jar, but in the main game, strong players tend to remain seated and weak players tend to be replaced, either by other weak players or by strong players who then move the median skill line higher still.

Thus we have the Brazil Nut Theory of Must-Move Games:

> Over time, the main game
> will emerge as the tougher
> game to beat.

Other factors reinforce this. For one thing, must-move games are always fed by players just starting their sessions.

These players may be nervous, distracted, or still preoccupied by events out there in the world. They haven't settled in yet, and they certainly haven't been in the game long enough to suss out the strengths and weaknesses of their foes. In the sense that any player just starting out his session is a little vulnerable, the must-move game always has a higher percentage, and a constantly refreshing universe, of new players who can be attacked on the basis of their newness alone. This combination of new money and potentially ill-defended money makes the must-move game generally softer and weaker than the main game.

Main games, on the other hand, quickly become "veteran" games, filled with players who have been seated for many hours, who have become comfortable and relaxed at the table, and who, if they have their wits about them, have acquired their clear gestalt. They've also accumulated some chips (as a function of the migration of money from weak players to strong ones), which makes them that much more confident, relaxed, and dominant. This situation will pertain until quite late at night when the universe of players becomes overly tired and their perception and judgment start to wane. At that point, these veterans become potential victims, but also at that point the must-move game has probably long since broken down.

Viewed through a different lens, we could say that a strong player in a must-move game is a big fish in a small pond. It can certainly be a cozy, comfortable pond, but alas it doesn't last. For all the time you're there, you work to control the game. You maneuver yourself to a favorable seat position. You project a tactically useful image. You acquire reads on your foes. You identify soft targets and attack them, including the stream of new players entering the game. All these edges disappear the instant the floor person says, "Main game, please."

Now you go to the main game and face a whole new set of challenges.

- You don't know your new foes, apart from the glimpse you got when they were back with you in the must-move game.
- You don't have optimum seating. You may in fact have the worst possible seat if a savvy player has just taken the opportunity of an open seat to move out from under a dangerous foe.
- You're facing entrenched money, and possibly big money, in the hands of relaxed opponents.
- You have no image.

Can you think of any other ways that the transition from must-move game to main game can work against you? Can you think of ways to make it work for you?

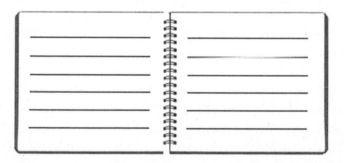

Here's one plus about moving: A new game is a fresh start. If your image in the must-move game was unfavorable, you have a chance to reinvent yourself now. Likewise, if your stack has gotten low, you can go ahead and reload when you move. Sometimes, though, when you move from the must-move game to the main game, you find a situation so adverse, a line-up so daunting, that it really makes no sense to stay in the game. Given the array of disadvantages you face, you might reasonably conclude that it's a game you cannot beat. You look longingly back over your shoulder at the sweet, soft, must-move game, and wish you could be back there. Alas, they don't call it "must-move" for nothing. You're stuck in the main game.

Or are you?

True, you can't return to the must-move game, but you can always shop for another game at a different limit—or even in a different casino. In some clubs, if you decline to play in the main game, they'll make you wait an hour and then put you back on the list for that limit. This will eventually recycle you back into the must-move game—if you're patient enough to wait.

And if you're not that patient, if you decide to tough it out in the main game, I would ask you to ask yourself why. Do you feel you can beat the game? You've already determined, by your best guess, that you cannot. So what is it then? Action? Perhaps you weren't in that must-move game all that long, and haven't yet quenched the thirst for poker that brought you to the club today. You haven't sufficiently scratched that itch.

If that's the case and you know it, fine, go ahead and scratch the itch. Just be prepared to pay the price: a seat in an unfavorable game against difficult foes. Wouldn't it be better to tear yourself away? Take a break. Good players, as we'll discuss in the next section, don't stay in situations where they don't have the edge, because they're there to make some money, not to scratch some itch.

Think about it the next time you're must-moved, and ask yourself, in all honesty, whether this is a game you can beat. If you decide not, decline the seat. Let some other lamb go to the slaughter instead. There's bound to be a better game for you out there somewhere, so long as you're patient enough, and clear-eyed enough, and strong-willed enough to go get it.

THE SEVEN HABITS

Perhaps you have read, or at least bookstore-browsed, Stephen Covey's *The Seven Habits of Highly Effective People*. This book has spawned a rash of follow-ups, including *The Seven Habits of Highly Effective Families* and *The Seven Habits of Highly Effective Teens*. So far as I know, we have yet to see *The Seven Habits of Highly Effective Felons* or *The Seven Habits of the Highly Effective Homeless,* but no doubt they're in the works. Meanwhile, being the type to leave no pop culture stone unturned, I now present seven habits of highly effective hold'em players.

1. They leave bad games. Good hold'em players know when they're in a game they can't beat. If they feel they're outclassed or outgunned, they're (wo)man enough to admit it. They don't regard retreat as defeat. Rather, they see it as a strategic redeployment of their time, talent, and bankroll. Acquire the habit of leaving unfavorable games and you will be money ahead—way ahead—in the long run.

How do you know when you're in the wrong game? Sometimes you don't, alas, until it's too late, and you find yourself and your stack under siege. Even from the outset, though, there are a number of clues and cues you can use to decide whether this game will be a generous host to your efforts. First, remember to look at the stack sizes. If there are several players with gargantuan mounds of chips, well, they didn't accrue those stacks by magic. Maybe they caught lucky or maybe they're running unusually good, but in either case you don't want to mess with them. Go find a softer target. Extending that principle to the entire table, you generally don't want to enter any game where your normal buy-in is less than the average stack size. You'll be on the defensive from the moment you sit down.

Mike Caro told us long ago that happy games are good

games. If people are laughing and talking and joking and having a jolly ol' time, they're not likely to be bringing their best laser-like focus to the task at hand. On the other hand, if the crew is dour, silent, intent, and intense, you'll find no obvious inattentiveness to exploit. Nor will you be able to work your image to the point where people are calling you loosely, and jovially giving you their chips. All other things being equal, gravitate toward games that look like a party, and stay away from the wakes.

As the game progresses, keep looking around the table, and keep track of how many genuinely superior players you face. You'll know they're superior if you find that you're reacting to their moves, rather than forcing decisions on them. If there are more than two such crafty, powerful players in the game, seek greener pastures. I know that some table-selection theorists argue that the presence in the game of known leakers or losers can more than compensate for the competition from other tough soldiers. I don't disagree with that, except to note that in many cases there are other games available that have abundant leakers and losers, but no other contenders for the top dog spot you seek to oc-cupy. Scout around. A game isn't truly good unless you're the best player in it.

What other cues or clues can you think of to warn your-self that the game you're in is not the best place to play?

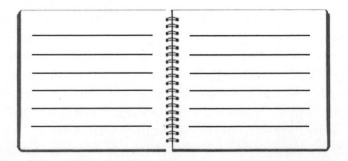

Don't forget to look for these clues or cues within. Look particularly for strands of denial that reveal your true understanding. If you find yourself thinking, "This game's not so bad," it's probably not so good. Are you trying to justify inertia? Don't be a victim of chair glue—move!

2. They take control. Good players have something in mind beyond winning a few bets and going home with some extra jangle in their pockets. Highly effective hold'em players are ones who to take control of the table. They lead, and make others follow. They destabilize their foes and force hard decisions, for they know that real success at the hold'em table comes from compelling others to make mistakes.

They achieve this goal, first of all, simply by setting it. Shockingly, the vast majority of hold'em players never ever have this aim in mind. They're content to wait for good cards (or chase with bad cards) and let the luck of the draw determine whether they quit winners. Good players, on the other hand, strive to be "the straw that stirs the drink." In service of this purpose, they adopt a style of play that might best be described as relentless. They love nothing better than to hear other players complain that they raise too much and push too hard. It's music to their ears.

Does this mean that maniacs are highly effective players? Sometimes they are, but that's really only by accident, since maniacs don't set out to be highly effective. Highly effective players, on the other hand, can often look like maniacs (we've defined them as Fakiacs), or various other species of bully, for this image allows them to play the sort of aggressive game they intend to play. Sometimes they do play too strongly, pushing edges that they don't actually have. But they never err on the other side. You may find a good player being cautious or cagey, but you'll never catch him being weak or meek or mousy.

Predictable players, players who frequently call and rarely raise, make other players feel right at home. The highly effective player doesn't want you to feel right at home. He won't let you get comfortable. He'll raise more than he'll call, check-raise frequently, and check-call rarely. He'll vary his play (but never veer too far from strong play) and he'll vary his image so that you're constantly in doubt about him and his style and intentions. He'll be tricky and frisky. He'll make you react to him. If he does his job right, you will react wrong.

Against this sort of player, paradoxically, tight players play too tight and loose players play too loose. The tight player decides to beat this guy by snugging up his starting requirements. This results in the tight player essentially removing himself from competition, leaving the power player that much more in command. Loose players, on the other hand, can't believe that the power player is not out of line, so they try to play back. Lacking the confidence, insight, and preparation to do the job right, they end up riding a roller coaster—riding, but not driving.

How can you take control of your hold'em game like this player does? First, of course, you must make it your objective. So many players play to *not lose.* They're satisfied to come home from the club saying, "Well, I broke even but I had a real good time." Do not be satisfied with that. Set out to terrorize the table, and if you reach a point where everyone is looking at you and wondering what you're going to do next, then you can feel like you've accomplished your goal.

Next, remove the word "call" from your vocabulary. It's a bit simplistic to suggest a policy of *raise or fold,* but on the other hand, if that were your plan you wouldn't go too far wrong. To take control of the game, you have to be ready to *drive,* and that means not just raising preflop but also frequently leading into the flop and the turn. You want to win more than your share of fold-outs, but your foes won't surrender unless you give them the chance. Bet. Bet again. If this sort of balls-out play makes you nervous, restrict your action to top-quality hands—but be the one to get the last raise in. Press hard to win big.

There have no doubt been times when you've felt completely on top of your game and completely in control of the table. Good players describe this as being "in the zone." Can you recall and record what it was like to be in the zone? How did you feel? What did you do right? What let you take over the table?

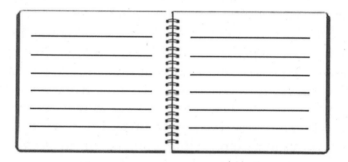

Having identified positive aspects of your past play, seek to carry those aspects into the next game you play. After all, the zone doesn't happen by accident.

3. They practice patience. Effective players know how to wait. They understand that everyone gets their fair share of good cards, and that a key to success is surviving until the good cards come. So even though they're super-aggressive when the opportunity presents itself, they know better than to force an opportunity that's not there. They recognize that some hold'em hands are like stiffs in blackjack; your job isn't to win with them, but to lose as little as possible. They'll drive hands like K-Q suited, for example, but not to the point of ignoring an ace on the flop. They're strong, not suicidal.

You may see one of these players going so long between hands that he seems to be a rock or a fossil. In reality, he's just enduring a steady stream of jackthrees and stupid connectors without losing his patience or his poise. He's like a rattlesnake coiled to strike—and sunning himself on the rocks in the meantime.

Nor will he jump into a game that's just not right. He doesn't need the buzz that badly. If his only choice is to play at a limit higher than he's used to, or against a lineup he doesn't like, he'll simply wait instead. You'll find him in the coffee shop doing a crossword puzzle (or studying a poker book) until a favorable situation presents itself. You'll never find him deluding himself into thinking that he can "survive in this game" until the good game comes available. You probably won't find him playing down, either, slumming at the lower limits to kill time while his initials climb the sign-up board. He knows he can't play his best when the money isn't meaningful, and he's not going to squander his limited poker focus and energy in a game that offers inadequate return.

There's a certain diffidence about this guy. He almost doesn't seem to care whether he plays or not. If he's at the table or away from the table, in the hand or out of the hand, it's all pretty much the same to him. In the name of practicing patience he is taking the longest possible view of the game. He knows that nothing matters but making as many correct decisions as possible, and that one of the best decisions he can make is *don't play now:* don't join that table; don't enter this pot; don't call these raises. He waits. He is content to wait.

The patient player knows that playing hold'em can trigger within him certain predictable biochemical responses. He knows that being in action at the poker table will prompt the release of adrenaline, endorphins . . . a whole cranial cocktail within. He acknowledges that some of these neuro-chemicals make him feel good, and realizes that on some level this is part of the reason he plays. But he's no slave to internal narcotics. He's here to *play well,* not to *feel good,* and his clarity of purpose allows him to wait and wait and wait without becoming antsy or, as a function of having to wait, feeling that the world is somehow unfair.

Many impatient players can't resist the cranial cocktail. They surrender to action. This creates a new problem, for now they start to see themselves as weak, unable to control their own will—or their *won't,* as the case may be. They will then frequently attempt to distract themselves from these uncomfortable revelations. How? By playing more hands! Yes, it's true: Impatient people become *more* impatient in order to escape the fact of their own impatience. The pa-tient player doesn't have this problem. He knows he's in control and he feels good about himself, so he's content to dwell in his own presence until the circumstances of the game call upon him to act. He doesn't use poker to distract himself from himself. He doesn't have to.

Bottom line: The patient player knows he can beat the game—and knows he doesn't have to beat it every hand.

What five things could you do to improve your patience quotient?

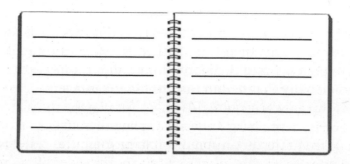

4. They play the players. "I've been sitting here for two solid hours," goes the familiar lament, "and I haven't won a single hand. What do you have to do to rake a pot around here?" Well, what you have to do—and effective players know this—is become involved in hands where you don't need cards to win. As we've noted before, if you have to have good cards to win, you *can't* win, not in the long run and not against tough foes. In addition to good cards, you need good attentiveness and a keen eye for opportunity. The highly effective hold'em player is always on the lookout for this opportunity, and he doesn't much care which two cards he holds when opportunity knocks. His attentiveness extends beyond gross characterizations such as weak/strong or loose/tight. He looks for *nuance* in a foe's approach to the game, holes through which he can punch a bet or pull a pot. He may notice, for example, a certain foe's tendency to fold in the face of a check-raise. If he spots that tendency, he'll launch a salvo at the appropriate moment, and won't worry at all about the cards he holds when he does. This is a case of playing the player, and it's something that good players do every day.

Where's the patience? you might ask. *How can the guy be practicing patience, but also looking for opportunities to launch naked bluffs?* The answer lies in his definition of the word *opportunity*. Your typical kosher poker player equates *opportunity* with *good cards*. The highly effective player equates *opportunity* with *good cards or good situation*. He has broadened his definition, but not forced it. He doesn't make rash moves into unknown foes. Rather, he schools himself on his opponents, and then looks for moments of weakness or predictability that he can turn to his advantage.

How can you acquire this knack for playing the players? No sweat . . . you have it already. On your best days, you have good innate reads on many of your foes, either because they're terribly easy to read or because you happen to be extra attentive. These reads may be so subtle or intangible that you might not be able to put them into words. Highly effective players don't need to put their reads into words. Their intuitive database, if you will, serves them sufficiently well that they know which moves to make when, and against whom. If your intuitive database is not so powerful, learn to articulate your reads. When you see something meaningful at the poker table, don't just note it in a vague, general sense—put it into words. You needn't go so far as to write down what you've seen (though that wouldn't hurt) but do compose sentences like this in your head:

> *Seat one telegraphs his intention to fold.*
> *Seat two tries to look at seat one's cards.*
> *Seat three raises with middle pairs in early position.*
> *Seat four plays bad aces.*
> *Seat five traps.*
> *Seat six (that's me!) never stops paying attention.*
> *Seat seven chickens out on the turn.*
> *Seat eight can be driven off his draws.*
> *Seat nine is drunk.*

Naturally gifted players get great intuitive reads, but not every effective player is naturally gifted. Some just work hard. They never stop studying their foes, and they never stop assembling and updating a matrix of behaviors, betting patterns, and cards shown. If these correlations seem complex or opaque to you, you can render everything simpler and clearer just by saying (silently) what you see. Tell yourself—literally *tell yourself*—what's going on around you. The willingness and ability to be very detailed about your discoveries will overcome a lack of natural gifts.

In fact, screw ability. Mostly it just takes willingness. You must be willing to work relentlessly at deciphering your foes, and then be willing to put your reads boldly into play. It's not enough to know that the blind won't defend, for example, if you'll still only raise when you've got great cards. That blind is there for the taking—your observations tell you so—so don't be shy: Go get it!

Describe a situation in which you won, or could win, or next time *will* win, without holding any special cards at all.

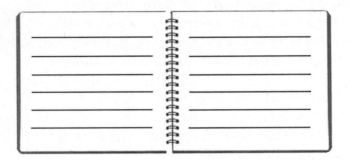

5. They keep records. This is old news, but it bears repeating: Highly effective hold'em players track their results. They know how many hours they have played and how much money they've won and lost over the last week, month, year, decade. They know whether they do better in short sprints or marathon sessions. They can identify the limits that are most profitable—and most leaky. They know not to trust these numbers explicitly or exclusively, for short-term fluctuation has a way of rendering statistics meaningless. But they also know that the attention they pay to their performance actually *helps* their performance. Beholden to themselves to be frank about their outcomes, they do their best to wrest outcomes they can be proud of.

If a player doesn't keep track of his results, he's apt not to be highly effective, for two reasons. First, he has no way of knowing what limits, locales, and times of day he has historically been most or least successful, so he can't know where to go to maximize his opportunity or minimize his risk. Second, if he's not keeping score it's probably because he can't stand to face the sad fact of his losing record. He talks himself into thinking that he's generally successful, even though he has no hard evidence to back up the claim. This self-delusion is de facto the mark of an ineffective player. He is not honest. He doesn't acknowledge his holes. How can he be effective?

You keep records, right? You log your sessions in and out, note how much you won or lost, and at what limit you played and for how long. As I've said before, individual outcomes don't matter. So you lost during this last session, or even the last five sessions in a row. Doesn't matter. All that matters is going home and recording that information faithfully and honestly, and then analyzing the information to see what you can glean. Are you playing so many hours that you become fatigued? Are you playing beyond your bankroll? Or could it be that you're playing so small that you can't take the game seriously? Should you even be playing hold'em in the first place (your seven-card stud results having been consistently superior)? Whether you can extract meaningful information from your records or not, you will prosper from the effort you make at extraction. You can't avoid it. Keeping and analyzing your records leads you naturally to a deeper, more articulate appraisal of your performance over time.

Highly effective players know the difference between *review* and *regret*. Regret is the useless ruing of adverse outcomes. *If only I'd hit my flush on the river, I'd have raked a monster pot and quit winners for the day!* Review is the thoughtful inspection of past play in search of alternate strategies and lessons to be learned. *I three-bet preflop with pocket jacks, and that put me in an exposed position on the flop. Perhaps I should have flat-called there, for deception if my hand looked good and for an easier escape if I had to bail.*

Meditate for a moment on the distinction between review and regret, and think of times when you've experienced either or both brands of thought.

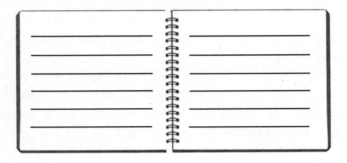

Learn to review without regret and you're halfway toward keeping meaningful records. For more on the subject, including sample logs and software sources, please see the relevant section of my book *Killer Poker: Strategy and Tactics for Winning Poker Play.* Or just open a notebook or spreadsheet and start keeping score.

Because the game doesn't count if you don't keep score.

6. They play good cards. Something happens to certain hold'em players once they start to get good. Having learned how to read their foes, and how to turn those reads into profitable plays, they forget (for a while at least) the foundation upon which their successful hold'em game is built. They forget (for a while at least) Mike Caro's immortal observation that "hold'em is a game of high cards." They forget (for a while at least) that most of their muscular moves require at least a little bit of actual factual muscle. Awed by the strength of their image, their reads, and their handsome, chiseled features, they get reckless and careless and sloppy, and their bottom line suffers accordingly.

Case in point: A fairly good hold'em player has just graduated to the middle limits. Much to his surprise, he finds that the quality of play there is not much higher than what he left behind at the so-called "upper low limits" ($5–$10, $6–$12, $9–$18). More to the point, he discovers that he can move players off their hands with turn bets or raises. He comes to believe that he can "outplay them on later streets." What he doesn't realize is that he tightened up when he moved up, so that he was generally making those turn bets or raises with superior hands—and his foes accurately read him for the hands he had. He didn't outplay them so much as outgun them. Nevertheless, he comes to see himself as a master of post-flop play. His own high opinion of himself carries him away completely. Now instead of raising preflop with quality big cards and big pairs, he's banging away with hands like T-9 suited, rationalizing his rash action with the soothing belief that he'll beat 'em on the flop or the turn or the river.

But his opponents are no dummies. They note that Mr. Wonderful has loosened up his starting requirements, and is routinely getting out ahead of his hand. Armed with this knowledge, they may now use a couple of effective countermeasures. They can either play back at him, knowing that he's into the hand with inferior values, or simply wait for major holdings and let him break himself upon the rocks of their superior hands.

It's a common evolution for hold'em players on the way up. They become better players, which leads to a spike in confidence. Confidence breeds looseness. Starting requirements take a tumble, reckless adventures ensue, and the would-be Killer Poker player experiences a setback.

Great players pass through this phase and emerge on the other side. It's not that they go back to being tight, frugal, hit-to-win players. Rather, they discover a happy medium between knowing how to win without good cards and simply waiting to have them. They don't ignore opportunities to capture pots with steals and stone bluffs, but they don't force those opportunities either. They constantly work their image, feigning friskiness so that their good hands get paid off, but they don't get taken in by that image themselves. They've mastered the trick of *looking* out of line while not *being* out of line.

This leads to a great existential quandary of hold'em: Why is one player's reckless adventure another player's masterful deception? How can T-9 suited be unplayable trash one hand but a major holding the next? The answer lies in hold'em's anthem of equivocation, "It depends." It depends on who's holding the cards, who's up against him, his position and table image, and a whole host of other factors that expert players weigh and measure with a jeweler's precision and a dancer's grace. Top players *do* get out of line, but only on their own terms, and only with full knowledge of themselves and their foes. They don't forget the immutable mathematical certainty that 7-2 offsuit is a 9-1 underdog to pocket aces, but they know that sometimes— though rarely—this doesn't matter. Above all, they don't get carried away with themselves.

I once heard a theory about cockroaches. Since roaches routinely develop resistance to every new pesticide we throw at them, it seems that the only sure way to kill them is by direct pulverization—stepping on them. Given this, and given their crafty nature, it may be that cockroaches will eventually develop the ability to appear to be two or three inches to the left or right of where they actually are, so that when you stomp on them you miss.

Great hold'em players have mastered a similar art. They know that there's no substitute for a massive hand, but when you can hold 7-2 offsuit and make it look like pocket aces, you have the best of all possible worlds.

What hands do you play? If you've never done this exercise, do it soon: Play your next session with notebook in hand and record each and every holding you saw fit to back with a bet.

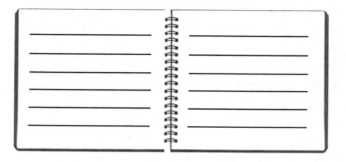

Maybe the mere fact of having to record that you played 9-6 suited will wean you from the habit of playing it at all.

7. They see things as things are. The highly effective hold'em player is immune to wishful thinking. If he holds 8-8 when the flop comes pure wheelhouse and bettors swarm into the pot like hiving honey bees, he knows it's time to let go. He knows that no amount of yearning will turn his two-outer into anything better than a two-outer—one that may be drawing dead. He doesn't waste time lamenting the flop that might have been. His perception is not degraded by such noise.

The highly effective hold'em player is immune to disappointment. When he flops K♠-Q♠-7♦ into his J♠-T♠ holding, only to see the turn and the river come clang-clang, he knows that his only options are to bluff or fold. If he bluffs it's because he thinks there's a decent chance of success, not because he feels his draw deserves better than it got. He has no need to compound misery by throwing bets after regrets.

The highly effective hold'em player is immune to resentment. He doesn't take it personally when someone attacks his blind. He assumes that his foe has a valid strategic reason for that action, and he will react with a valid strategic response. He may feign fury in order to get loose calls from those who think they've put him on tilt, but he stays serene in his core. He has no interest in petty vendettas. Nor does he blame the dealer for turning certain cards, any more than he'd blame his watch for telling him it's midnight.

The highly effective hold'em player knows no superstitions. He agrees with Branch Rickey that "luck is the residue of design." If seat three is "lucky" for him, that's only because seat four is weak and seat two is strong. If the Rabbit's Foot Casino is "lucky" for him, that's only because he knows there's generally a soft lineup waiting for him there at this time of the day or this day of the week. If a certain dealer is "lucky" for him, it's only because his distracting banter with that dealer puts other players off their guard. He doesn't mind talking about how lucky he is, for he knows it doesn't hurt to have other players think he's thus blessed, but he'd never call himself unlucky because he'd never want a foe to entertain that inspiring idea.

The highly effective player never gets too high or two low. He doesn't gamble to get even or get well. He doesn't feel fear or urgency or need. He tends his tranquility and monitors his state of mind. His goal is to be completely transparent to the information he's receiving at the poker table, and he knows that any emotional or perceptual interference on his part will block his efforts to see things as they are. He doesn't give a damn about *what if*, only about *what is*.

Some things get under everybody's skin, but what bothers me at the poker table may not bother you, and vice versa. Generate a list of things that *really piss you off*. Can you imagine that having such a list will limit the negative impact of these peeves?

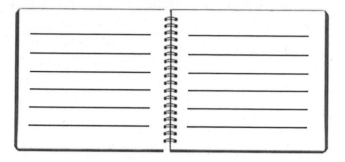

Well, there you have it. Better than any boy scout, highly effective hold'em players are *discerning, strong, patient, observant, diligent, selective,* and *clear.* They have, of course, many more than these seven helpful habits. Among others I can think of:

> *They don't play drunk. They do play rested. They have adequate bankrolls for their limit. They have avid outside activities and interests. They get their exercise. They eat right. They study the game. They talk poker with knowledgeable friends. They take bad outcomes in stride. They love.*

Down on the level of the play of hands:

> *They attack new money. They save bets on the river by not bluffing the unbluffable. They don't call when they know they're beaten. They don't play sheriff. They don't throw cards or fits or tantrums. They put foes on hands and play accordingly.*

What else can you think of that players who do well do?

Which of those habits already exist within you? Which do you plan to add?

UPS AND DOWNS

We've talked a lot in this book about the play of certain types of very aggressive players. Whether they're maniacs, Fakiacs, or bullies, they have a common tendency to push the bet structure outside the typical player's comfort zone. They do this by raising instead of calling and by pressing thin edges. Though they sometimes give away equity by betting with the worst of it, they gain that equity back by taking control of the game. Specifically, they win more than their share of fold-outs, and therefore, their (let's be charitable and call it *liberal*) style of play pays for itself.

This sort of high-fluctuation, high-variance game can be very disconcerting to stable, sensible players whose strategy of waiting for good cards and betting for value serves them best in low-variance games. It is often these straightforward, sensible-but-cautious players who suffer most at the hands of a roller-coaster rider like the Mad Cow or Stanley Steemer. So let's take a look at the high-variance phenomenon and see if we can find a way to feel more at home among the hopelessly (or anyway, the seemingly) deranged.

Here's a graphic representation of a strong-tight hold'em player's hold'em session.

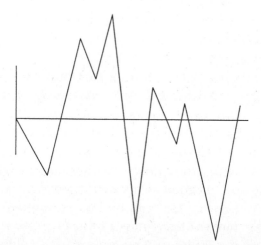

As you can see, this is a player who experiences relatively modest ups and downs. He doesn't swing too far from even, and he likes it that way, because much as he loves to win, he hates to lose, and he'll play tight and snug, and sacrifice the potential for a big win to hold at bay the demon—that's how he sees it, as a demon—of a big loss.

Now let's look at a high-variance player's session.

Quite a different picture. This is a player who experiences extreme swings. He'll go way up and way down, but at the end of the day, at least in this example, he finishes up pretty much the same as the snug player does. Today may or may not be a representative day, but today they both broke about even.

And they both achieved their goal, which was notionally to make money, but really to have the kind of session they each wanted to have. A snug player wants a snug session. A volatile player wants a volatile session. Each may believe that his or her strategy is a winning one, and each may believe that the strategy serves the money goal. Really what the strategy serves is comfort. Tight players feel comfortable in low-variance games. That's why high variance is such an effective weapon against them; it discomfits them. Loose players, on the other hand, feel at home in loose games. They like to four-bet it preflop with K♣-9♣. Not only is it their idea of a good time, they fervently believe (perhaps correctly) that playing the game on their terms is the way for them to win big. On the other hand, they can't stand to be in games where there's not enough action. They may profit, but they won't be mentally engaged. Since it's not the scariest roller coaster ride in the park, it's not the one they want to be on.

High-variance players have little trouble turning up the volume on a low-variance game. They simply start throwing out bets until someone takes the bait. Eventually someone must take the bait, or else the high-variance player will run all over the game. The low-variance player will have more difficulty turning down the heat on a high-variance game. His only weapon is his own tight play, and that's a passive weapon that his high-variance opponent can easily ignore. The low-variance player soon finds that he doesn't like his options. He doesn't want to play too tight, and miss out on the maniac's money. He doesn't want to play too loose and join the bully on a highway to hell. What he wants—what he can't have—is his quiet little game back.

I would encourage such a player to glance back at those graphs and note this: Even though the high-variance player has higher highs and lower lows, he still passes through zero, just like the low-variance player does. Whether his climbs and falls are short or long, he still climbs and he still falls. What the low-variance player needs to do, then, is to recognize that while the amplitude of his game may be changed by high-variance tactics, the outcome remains the same: Good play and good cards will win; bad play and bad cards will lose. In the short term, the wins and losses will seem greater, but that's only a function of magnified spikes. In the long run, the outcomes will be exactly the same.

Is this true? Are outcomes really the same in the long run? Well, yes, if you extend the sum of your poker sessions to the final moment of your life. You can't take it with you, after all. As the saying goes, "you're born broke, you die broke, everything else is just fluctuation." This may be cold comfort to the working pro, but it's a fact nonetheless.

A snug player in a loose game has difficulty adjusting, for he feels that participating in the volatility will hurt his bottom line. However, if he fails to adjust he'll make errors that definitely hurt his bottom line. Thus we arrive at a paradox:

> To improve your bottom line, you must ignore your bottom line.

To play properly in a high-variance game, a low-variance player must absolutely drag his eye away from his stack. He must absolutely trust that he'll still pass through zero on a regular basis. He must see the higher highs and lower lows for the mirages they are: special conditions brought about by special circumstances. If he is not prepared to ignore the extreme tidal rise and fall of his chip stack, then he must leave the game. He has no other choice. His preoccupation with variance will cause him to make mistakes—real mistakes that will cost him real money.

Example one: A low-variance player in a high-variance game finds himself holding A-K, exactly the sort of hand he'd drive in a low-variance game, and exactly the sort of hand he wants to be in there with now. But the flop comes ace-free and king-free, and the betting doesn't slow down. On a flop of 9-8-3, there's a bet and a raise and a call before the action gets to him. He assumes that the post-flop action indicates two-pair or sets out against him, and fears he's nearly drawing dead. He has forgotten what sort of game he's in. He has forgotten that high-variance has skewed both hand values and pot size. People will bet draws and naked pairs, and calls that would be incorrect in a smaller game are correct here. But our hero doesn't want to get stuck for a bunch of chips, so he mucks. Having joined the preflop festivities, he now picks exactly the wrong time to get tight.

Example two: Our hero now finds himself with pocket queens in late position and, with help from the field, drives the pot up to its maximum. Five players see the flop for four bets apiece. Now the flop comes K-A-5. In a low-variance game, our hero would have generally only committed two bets to this pot preflop, because other players wouldn't have been so eager to help him bet it up. He would have looked at that ace and that king, judged himself to be beaten, and gotten away from his hand. In this game, though, he's got four bets committed, and his commitment colors his judgment. He reminds himself that the players here don't always have real hands when they bet, so he looks at a bet and a raise and a call in front of him on the flop and concludes, *Hell, they're all bluffing!* There's a huge difference between betting into an ace-free and king-free flop, and betting into one that contains both. Our hero does not at this moment discern the difference, and calls along, because the pot is a monster and all those chips temporarily blind him to the danger that the ace and the king pose. Somewhere along the line he realizes that he probably needs to hit his queen to win. In the worst telling of the tale he *does* hit his queen—and loses to someone holding J-T.

As you can see, the logic of calling in the second case is exactly opposite to the logic of folding in the first. Yet both types of (flawed) logic are present in the player who doesn't know how to handle high variance. And both types of mistake have the same root cause: He is afraid to lose big. While attempting to mix it up with these hyperactive bettors, he's also trying to protect himself from variance. He becomes confused. He folds when he should call, chases when he should fold, and ends up wondering how anyone can ever beat a game with maniacs in it.

Here's how: Get out on top. Given that you will experience higher highs and lower lows, simply stop playing when you reach a higher high, thank the game for giving you a nice profit, and go hunt down a comfy little low-variance game where you can use your sound basic strategy to grind out a win. It's axiomatic that the roller coaster will take you up and down. Simply get off at the top.

To pull off this nifty trick, just follow these three simple steps:

1. Get used to high variance. Recognize that hands you'd play for one or two bets in a quiet game you'll have to play for three or four bets in this loud one.
2. Get aggressive with big hands and big draws. You will

need to hit to win, but when you do hit, you'll hit for a sizeable sum.

3. Get out while the getting is good. A high-variance game presents a tempting invitation to piss away your profits. Decline the invitation.

This last point is the point to focus on. Big pots can beguile the mind. If you win a monster pot or two, you're sure as hell going to like how it feels, and you're sure as hell going to want to win another one or two. You'll be playing hit-to-win with extremely dubious holdings like 8-7 offsuit. You'll look at any pocket pair and think about the mighty, mighty set you can flop. When that happens you're just another roller coaster rider. Eventually you'll pass back through zero and wonder where your chips wandered off to. What goes up must come down. Get out before it all comes down on you—unless you've got the game sussed out, of course. But in that case, in the case where you've become comfortable with the wild ride, then you're no longer a low-variance player looking to protect himself in a high-variance game. Now you're a high-variance player looking to maximize his edge against timid players who can't adjust.

MOVES

Here comes a menu of hold'em moves you can use from time to time. None of these moves works without fail. Some require an almost perfect harmonic convergence of foes, image, and cards. None are unknown to expert players, and I don't imagine they're all that foreign to you. What may not yet be part of your thinking is the whole idea of *making moves* as a means of bootstrapping your game to a loftier plane of play. When your strategic approach to hold'em is limited to "What do I do with these cards?" there's really not much room for growth. However, when you change your orientation to "What sort of moves can I make here?" you're thinking about the game at a higher quantum level. Many of your foes will never reach this level. Some can't even conceive of it. The ones you need to respect are the ones who are already up there, hurling moves down on you.

The Thoughtful Check. Sometimes you're in early position and you'd really like to get a free card. A meek check, you realize, will probably induce a bet, but a loud and forceful check will look so transparently like a free-card grab that it will likely induce a bet as well. How about a thoughtful check? Call time. Study the board. Study your foes. Study your cards. Make it look like you've got an authentically hard decision to make. You may not get the free card you're looking for, but then again you might. If your foe is on the fence about betting, your own indecision may persuade him to avoid betting into the check-raise he fears you may be contemplating.

Some players disdain this sort of coffeehousing. They figure that your actions are your actions, no matter how you dress them up. If you have a tendency to check and fold, they know that already. If you're capable of check-raising, they figure they know that too. All of this is true as far as it goes, but it doesn't go quite far enough. How do they know these things about you? By observing your past actions. By correlating your tells with your decisions. In other words, by putting a read on you. Maybe you can't prevent this from happening, but why not confuse the issue? Blowing a little smoke, such as pausing to ponder a check you've already decided to make, may have the effect of undermining your foe's confidence in his read. At minimum it will do no harm.

And look at the sort of opportunity you might create. Suppose you make a thoughtful check, and your pause causes your foe to pause and ponder, too. What is he thinking now? That you're trying to deceive him by feigning either strength or weakness. Weakness, he finally decides, figuring that you'll fold. But you have gauged his uncertainty and now put *him* on a steal. He bets to win the pot—but you raise! Now his worst suspicion is confirmed. You hemmed and hawed to disguise the real power of your hand and to set up this trap—the very trap he has just fallen into. Now he folds, congratulating himself for, if nothing else, making you reveal the true strength of your hand. What we're talking about is using nuance that you yourself generated to finesse a pot away from your foe.

Perhaps you're familiar with the phrase "Make the latest possible decision based on the best available information." Sometimes a provocative action on your part, even an unusually slow or thoughtful check, will pop loose some information you otherwise wouldn't have had. If nothing else, it moves you out of your behavioral ruts, in which you may be unknowingly, dismayingly easy to read.

F.E.A.R.—Future Events Appear Real. Certain of your foes feel like they're cursed. Bad luck has afflicted them and they expect it to strike again. These foes will give you a *predictive tell,* which lets you anticipate how they'll react to the fall of certain cards—which you can then use against them. In the simplest terms, against a foe filled with F.E.A.R., play certain draws as if you own them. If the draw gets there, your chosen victim will experience a momentary lapse of reason. With his judgment temporarily clouded by a sense of *Here we go again!* he won't pause to consider that you're betting a hand you don't have. He'll just see himself as damned unlucky once again, and fold his hand without a second thought. Why would he call? He put you on a draw, and the draw got there.

You can help reinforce this set of mistaken assumptions by "betraying" yourself with a betting pattern consistent with the draw you aren't on. For instance, suppose you're heads up against one such Gloomy Gus and looking at a flop of T-9-8 rainbow. If he bets, go ahead and raise. Figure he's got top pair, good kicker. He, meanwhile, figures you for a naked jack or a 7. You're not actually looking to hit a scare card on the turn. You're hoping to hit a brick and have your opponent check, *so that you can check, too*. He'll conclude that your raise on the flop was a foreclosure raise, and will now firmly put you on the straight draw. If the river comes scary, his own evaluation of your hand has to put you on a straight or top pair. Skittish as he is, he *knows* he's beaten. He checks, you bet, he folds. Happy outcome. All because your foe feels snakebit and because you played the hand in a way that let him put you firmly on a hand that beats him.

If you should be unfortunate enough to "hit" your hand on the turn, you can still carry this gambit through by checking behind your foe. If he checks the river, you bet; if he bets, you raise. Either way he'll conclude that you made your hand on the turn, but figured he'd fold if you bet, so you checked in order to induce a bluff on the river. To a player with this kind of dour outlook, your bet on the turn would have looked very much like a steal. But checking the turn and betting or raising the river is consistent with a trap, not a bluff, and that's where your foe will put you.

Similarly, suppose you're in the big blind and it's folded around to the button, who makes a real estate raise. A call from you here can be consistent with a medium ace. Keep this in mind, because this is the hand you want him to put you on. Now here comes a flop of 9-7-8. Not much of anything for anyone. You check, he bets, you call. What does this tell him? That you have a weak piece of the flop, or overcards, or a bit of both with something like A-8 or A-7.

The turn is a 2, and nothing seems to have changed. You check. Your foe checks too, because he's feeling star-crossed and he doesn't want to bet again into a pot that you've demonstrated you won't be bluffed off of. (What does he hold here? Since he made a real estate raise preflop, he could have as little as nothing at all.) The river comes an ace, and you gleefully bet out. Your opponent knows there's no point in calling . . . you obviously hit your hand! He'll feel cursed that an ace fell on the river, but also (incorrectly) smug for making a good laydown in the face of a bad outcome.

Yes, I know he could have raised on the button with a good ace. Do *you* know that he'll raise on the button with other hands? If you do, you can make this move; otherwise, save it for a time when you're more sure. In all events, this whole class of play requires a foe you can steer. It's not like they're not out there—weak-minded players abound. Just make sure it's the right kind of weak mind. You need someone who's feeling like a loser, but not so much like a loser that he's past the point of pain. You want him to be dumb enough to conclude he's beaten, but smart enough not to play sheriff on you. It's a fine line, but a profitable one—one you prepare for, needless to say, by studying your foes intently when you're not involved in the hand.

Naked Ace Raisers. Some people think it's correct to raise under the gun or in early position with hands like A-9 or A-8 suited. They may be serving the larger purpose of bullying the table, or they may think their foes won't fight, but they are, in this instance at least, out ahead of their hands. They're hoping that their early position raise will make their hand seem stronger than it is, and allow them to steal the pot on any scary flop. We label these players *naked ace raisers*, or NARs, and devise a strategy to deal with them accordingly.

First, recognize that NARs don't make early position raises with naked aces only. They may be pushing middle pairs, or Q-J suited, or some other substandard hand. In most cases they're counting on their own post-flop aggression to carry the day. Knowing this, vary your play by simply calling with hands you might otherwise three-bet. Assume that you have the best hand (unless and until circumstances suggest otherwise). From here you can flat-call many flops and take the pot away on the turn. Since your enemy is out ahead of his hand, he often can't afford to follow through on his plan. He was hoping to face no opposition on later streets, but your strategically placed resistance thwarts his scheme.

Obviously, this play only works if you know who your NARs are. Presumably you have been tracking their play all along, so you know that they're not true value players, but rather frisky types prone to this sort of overplay. Even if they don't do it habitually, they may do it situationally when, for instance, they've just been the victim of a bad beat or suckout. So be on the lookout for a sudden spike in a foe's fury. The right combination of his out-of-position, out-ahead-of-his-hand play and your keen knowledge of his tendencies can create a profitable opportunity for you.

A caveat: Don't see NARs who aren't there. As we become more sophisticated in our own hold'em play, we start to imagine that everyone around us is sophisticated too, and as capable as we are of overbetting a hand from time to time. This may very well be true, but it may also be a rationalization we use to launch reckless adventures. Telling ourselves that we're not going to let some bloody-minded NAR push us off a pot, we get involved with substandard junk of our own, only to find ourselves facing big pairs or big paint and going off for many bets. With the following rule of thumb you can't go too far wrong.

> Treat all foes as straightforward
> until proven tricky.

Also recognize that if you're a NAR (and I'm not telling you you shouldn't be) there will come a time when your foes catch on and start to play back. Don't fear this; rather, plan for it. As we've already discussed, most foes will put you on a style of play (straightforward or bluffy) until you paint the opposite picture for them. As soon as you know you've been tabbed for NAR, simply gear down and wait for a premium hand. Since your foes have seen you being frisky, they'll assume you're being frisky next time too, and pay you off accordingly.

Come, Call, Chase, Fold. There's a certain type of player who has a certain happily predictable betting pattern. Typically a lemmy or a wally, he'll *come* into the pot with anything, *call* on the flop with any draw, *chase* against the odds on the turn, and *fold* on the river when he misses. Find yourself up against this foe, and you've got another opportunity to push and punish for profit.

The CCCFer is not exactly blind, but close to it. He doesn't evaluate any hand except his own, and doesn't do a particularly good job of that. He just wants to play, and considers a drawing hand as good as any made hand. Falling in love with his draws, he'll call along all the way to the river. The key to playing against the CCCFer is knowing that he'll fold if he misses. Why is this so important? Because, after all, most of the time he *will* miss. Confirmation bias tells us otherwise, but confirmation bias is wrong. If a draw is 3-1 against completing, it will fail to complete 75 percent of the time. Given the simple math of this, the more you attack the CCCFer, the more money you will make.

To exploit the opportunity presented by this player, you'll need to be three things: attentive, aggressive, and friendly.

Be attentive. Know that a given foe is the type to get married to his draws, but also not the type to assume (or recognize) that other players bluff. A straightforward player, he might even help educate you by complaining about all the good draws he's seen peter out. (It never hurts to ask what he had.) Or he may give himself away by consistently raising his draws on the flop, but checking on the turn if he doesn't improve, and then of course folding on the river if he fails to connect. This is a good player to watch instead of watching the cards fall. He'll be keenly focused on the board, looking for that precious straight card or flush card, and he won't be particularly vigilant against giveaway tells.

Be aggressive. Once you've put your foe on a draw, pour on the heat. Your goal is to get him heads up if you can, for two reasons. First, if he's one on one against you, his drawing odds are that much worse. Second, you want to be able to bet him off the pot at the river without any unwelcome involvement from third or fourth parties. It does you no good to bluff out your intended victim only to have a modest real hand call you down and beat you. Look for a strategic seat change that will put this opponent on your right, so that you can routinely raise his loose calls and seek to isolate against him.

Be friendly. This is the tricky part. Remember that your foe has twin goals for the hand: He wants to hit his draw and he wants to win the pot. You need to convince him that the two goals are inextricably linked, that if he misses his draw there's no way he can win the pot. You want, in other words, to keep him from thinking that even his busted draw might be good against your stone bluff. Make your river bet "more in sorrow than in anger." Create the impression that you're sympathetic of his draw that didn't get there, but, well, you have no choice but to bet your hand. From time to time, of course, you'll have a real hand, and if he folds don't be shy about showing him your winners. Accompany your reveal with a softly spoken "Good laydown," and reinforce in his mind the notion that he should throw away all his busted draws without a second thought.

All skilled hold'em players have moves such as these in their bag of tricks. They know which foes they can trap and which foes they can bully. They have their program betting strategies and their steal-raise requirements. As your own learning curve continues to rise, pay close attention to the moves you develop, accumulate, and use. The difference between making moves and not making them is one thing that distinguishes expert players from the dull normals. With this in mind, can you think of any moves you've developed (or observed and stolen) that continue to serve you well?

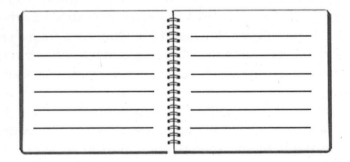

CAUTIONS

Having spent some time looking at moves we might make to exploit weaknesses in others, let's take a few moments to note some warnings of weakness, or leakness, in our own play. I'm not saying that you're guilty of any of the following missteps, but if you have been, do yourself the favor of acknowledging these lapses. This is the first step toward redressing them and removing them from your play.

Virtual Chips. A sad thing you see from time to time is someone who is buying into a game for short money (say $60 in a $6–$12 game) giving cash to a chip runner, "playing behind" until his chips arrive, and losing the entire sum before he even gets it! I don't imagine that you've ever done this sad thing, but can you imagine doing it? And can you imagine the mindset of someone who falls into this trap?

The problem isn't really the $60 lost—people lose $60 on a hand of hold'em every minute of every day. The problem is the psychological damage that the loss does to the person who suffers it. Imagine having the chip runner return to the table with your 30 two-dollar chips, only to find you whipping out another three twenties and forking them over. Would you feel strong and secure? Would you feel prepared to play your best game from that point forward? Not likely. Talk about starting off on the wrong foot!

There are two steps you can take to avoid this problem. First, and fundamentally, never buy in short. It's a basic precept of Killer Poker, as I'm sure you know by now, that short money is scared money. You never want to be on the broadcasting end of that fear. Second, just wait until your chips arrive. There's definitely something unreal about betting chips you don't yet have. It may be that the feeling of unreality is so strong that you will make the mistake of calling with imaginary chips where you would have otherwise (sensibly) folded, rather than face pushing real chips into the pot. Also, the time you spend watching the other players and getting your first feel for the game while you wait for chips is time well spent. Further, a player who jumps into action the moment he sits down betrays his impatience to the rest of the table, and that's a big, fat, hairy tell. What's your hurry? Wait. Relax. Your chips will be coming along in a moment, and the game will still be there when they do.

We've already discussed the need to practice patience in poker, and we've also discussed the problematic nature of everyone's first forced bet. At the end of the day, I don't think it much matters whether you enter on the blind or wait and post behind, but I would say that whenever you decide to jump in, your strategic disadvantage will be minimized if you just wait awhile, feel yourself becoming present at the table, and get into action on your terms at the time of your choice.

At the same time, do be on the lookout for players who make this mistake. If they buy in short and dive in cold, they're revealing their impatience and lack of strategic awareness. In the long run, I'm much more interested in this type of tell than anything I might get off a player during the individual play of hands. If a move toward his chips indicates an intention to bet, that's one thing, and a useful thing no doubt. But if his moves at the table at the start of his session indicate a fundamental inability to practice patience, that's a much more lucrative tell I can exploit for as long as he stays in the game.

I'll Show Me! Your spouse comes home one day from shopping. She or he has bought the most hideous, impractical, overpriced sofa/motorcycle/carpet/computer you can possibly imagine. You think that the purchase was a huge, ponderous waste of money, and you say so. "Oh, yeah?" your spouse snaps back. "Well, what about all the money you spend on poker?" You don't bother pointing out that you're investing, not spending; you've been down this road before. You break off the argument before it goes ballistic, but it's on your mind later that day when you head down to the club. You carry it with you into battle. Maybe somewhere in a dark corner of your mind there's even a tiny motivation to lose—or at least a higher tolerance for losing than usual. After all, your spouse has shown a fabulous capacity to waste money, why should you be any different?

Those prone to this "I'll show me!" state of mind willfully commit self-destructive acts in the misguided hope or expectation that the damage they're doing to themselves is actually afflicting someone else. Other stimuli can trigger this sort of revenge-against-the-world response. Maybe you're being treated unfairly at work. Maybe your parents/children/ siblings are driving you crazy. Maybe you think you're only seeking a little peace and quiet, or alone time, or a distraction when you race off to play poker. That may seem benign enough—we all can use a little distraction from time to time. But it's hardly a reason for playing poker, and it hardly augers well for the success of your session. Worse, it may mask a deeper resentment, which will manifest itself in repressed anger, poor judgment, flawed decision-making and, ultimately, failure and loss.

As I write these words, two questions cross my mind. The first is, How can I be sure that this is anyone's problem but my own? Maybe I'm the only person in the world who has ever cut off his nose to spite his face. Further, even if I can be reasonably sure that other people feel the same way, what right do I have to pry their minds open and poke around inside there with my stick? I suppose I have no such right. But may I claim the privilege? Having seen the damage that such toxic thinking can do to my own performance and results, I offer the warning up to you for your inspection. You can own it or not as you see fit.

Whether you own it or not, certainly be on the lookout

for this attitude in others. Nobody is perfect, and some of your poker foes are about as far from perfect as they can get. As we've already seen, people arrive in poker halls with all sorts of flawed motivations. If someone shows up determined to shoot himself or herself in the foot, it means they are incapable of playing expertly or even adequately. They're presenting you with a profit opportunity you won't want to overlook.

If it makes you nervous to think about yourself on such a frank psychological level, I would point out to you that there's a strong benefit to doing so. The moment you can say to yourself, in all honesty, "Sometimes I play hold'em because I'm mad at XYZ," the anger of others will be revealed to you. Their dark emotions and flawed motivations will become apparent. In that instant, you'll know who is leaving their money unguarded; you'll know who you can beat.

The Hippocratic Oath tells doctors, "First do no harm." We might tell ourselves the same thing. First, make sure that you enter every hold'em session with a light heart, a clear head, and pure motivation. If you cannot do these things, simply save your play for another day. If you can enter the game with your head on straight, look for those who can't, for they will be the players you profit from the most.

Calling Raises with K-Q. Most players don't give a second thought to calling a single raise with K-Q, especially K-Q suited. Maybe they should, though. Let's take a look. We'll start by listing the types of hands players raise with in a typically frisky mid-limit hold'em game.

A-A	K-K	Q-Q	J-J	T-T	9-9
A-K	A-Q	A-J	A-T	A-x suited	
K-Q	K-J	Q-J	Q-T	J-T	

Obviously you're a huge underdog to the big pairs, but even if you're suited, you're an underdog to upper middle pairs and also to any suited ace. The only hands you dominate are K-J, Q-J, Q-T, and J-T (the hands, of all these hands listed, least likely to come in for a raise). Most of the time, then, you start out at a small-to-large disadvantage against the raiser. Knowing this, why doesn't everybody throw away that K-Q and save themselves the money and the aggravation? Maybe they look at that paint-paint holding and get excited by all the pretty colors. Maybe they figure with three kings and three queens left in the deck they'll catch at least one pair about a quarter of the time . . . though if there are many other players calling the raise, they might not pause to consider that a lot of their kings or queens may be dead. Nor will they contemplate the flops that contain a king or a queen but also an ace, leaving them severely threatened by the sort of good-ace hands that people raise with most.

If the flop comes little-little-little, you're down to overcard outs, and that's almost never a happy place to be. If the flop comes middle-middle-middle, you're looking at a board that hits suited connectors and hits middle pairs for sets. If there's an ace on the flop with no king or queen, you have to get away from this hand, especially in games where players are promiscuous in their play of aces. This leaves straight draws and flush draws for your K-Q to feel good about, and those draws are much less likely to be getting correct pot odds in the face of a pre-flop raise.

Does this mean that K-Q can never be played? Of course not. If you're in late position or in the blind and there's an early position raise and a bunch of callers, go ahead and play your K-Q—but play it for the drawing hand it is. On the other hand, if you're in last position against a single late position raiser with no other callers, you have to ask yourself how much grief you want to take with that pretty painted (but pretty tainted) hand. It costs you nothing to hurl the hand away, but it costs you plenty to be caught holding K-Q when your foe makes a sensible raise with A-K or A-Q. You'll find yourself tied to the hand and dragged to the river, at the cost of lots of bets, plus a little self-respect.

Don't get me wrong, I love K-Q. I love Big Maxx—K♣-Q♣—so much that I named it after my wife. But here's the thing: I love any K-Q much better as a raising hand than a calling one. As usual, it's a matter of control. If I call raises with K-Q, I can only control the hand with a perfect flop. However, if I raise an otherwise unraised pot with K-Q, I have open options. If the board flops my way, I can drive. If it doesn't, I may still be able to drive. Depending on my opponents and my image, I can bluff an ace I don't have, play strongly in search of overcards, or just bet 'em off with raw chip strength, none of which I can hope to do if I'm just calling along. That's the raiser's prerogative.

And that's why we say of K-Q, as of so many hold'em holdings, "Loose call bad, loose raise good."

Next time you go to play, set yourself the goal of playing your K-Qs differently. Raise a little more, fold a little more, and call a little less, especially in the face of a raise. Experience the satisfaction of making a laydown that most can't make. In any case, don't consider your K-Q holding to be an automatic playing hand. Just because you *can* play it profitably in many situations doesn't mean you *must* play it always.

Contempt. That which is admirable is hard to see in poker. Paragons of virtue are mostly conspicuous for what they don't do. They don't throw cards or criticize weak players or abuse dealers. That which is contemptible, on the other hand, is plentiful and obvious. Examples of bad behavior abound—and call attention to themselves—every day in the poker world. When we see other players acting rudely or superstitiously or self-destructively, it's hard not to feel contempt for them. After all, we're not like that: We would never use foul language. We would never slow-roll a big hand. We would never even ask for a deck change. When we see others engaged in these despicable or counterproductive behaviors, we can't help feeling disdain.

Well, so what's wrong with that? People misbehave, we don't, we feel superior to them. No problem, right? Wrong. In feeling superior to our foes we are also objectifying them. We are reducing them in our minds to something less than human beings . . . something less than adversaries. As a function of this lowered opinion, we run the risk of underestimating their skills as players. Our own contempt for our foes leaves us vulnerable to attack. They may be poor excuses for human beings, but that doesn't mean they don't know how to raise with good cards. If we devalue the strength of their character, we might also devalue the strength of their hands.

Poker, as we know, is a game of incorporating information into a decision-making matrix. We do our best job of this when we don't clutter incoming information with outgoing transmissions of our own. Our contempt, I would suggest, is a sort of white noise that can only jam our reception and make it harder to get a clear fix on our foes. Consider . . .

You're playing hold'em against a real—let's not mince words here—dickhead. For the last three hours, he's been mouthing off about the poor quality of the players, the dealers, the table service, even the television reception. You've tried to let his loathsome behavior roll off your back, but his rudeness has recently driven a couple of tasty fish from the game, and now you're playing short-handed. You know that your obnoxious foe is angry, but you are angry, too. You're angry that such a dirtbag should be allowed to spoil both your fun and profit. As a function of this anger, you decide to fight fire with fire. You're determined to be just as big an asshole as this asshole. Just one problem: You're not very good at it. The subsequent short-handed joust devolves into a battle of ill wills, a game of aggravated assault, and you can't hold up your end. Your foe is contemptible, but he still takes home your money.

Did he tilt you? Yes, and you helped. Your righteous indignation boiled over into blind fury; you got put off your game. Contempt, then, turns out to be not just useless and pointless but actively counter-productive. Your opponent doesn't feel your contempt, for he's immune to such disapprobation. But you feel it, and you suffer as a result.

It's a conundrum: Poker requires confidence to the point of arrogance, but arrogance equals a feeling of superiority, and superiority breeds contempt, an emotion we can't allow ourselves to feel. What we need to do, then, is to observe but not critique. Note that a player is angry, rude, stupid, or assholic, but try not to assign a value verdict to those qualities. Try not to feel self-righteous. Try not to feel anything at all. Just watch . . . listen . . . absorb. Give yourself the benefit of the clearest possible picture of your enemy's state of mind. Don't contaminate that picture with your own opinions. Your opinions don't matter here. Only your actions matter, and your actions will be closer to perfect if they remain untainted by judgment.

In fact, if you encounter an adversary for whom you feel nothing but contempt, you'd be well served to project the exact opposite feeling. Smother that foe with waves of validation. Do everything in your power to encourage him in his flawed, dark habits. Every moment that he plays in such a state is an opportunity for you to beat him, not with the same contemptible behavior, but with good, solid play.

The contempt you feel for another player can be an asset, for it alerts you to your foe's emotional weakness. Just make sure that you don't meet his emotional weakness with weakness of your own. Recognize that he is generally flawed, then identify specific flaws in his game and pick him apart with surgical precision. There'll be plenty of time to feel contempt for him when you're done.

Expensive Free Blinds. Sometimes the unraised blind can be a curse in disguise, for it may put us in the risky position of trying to profit from hands we would otherwise not have played in the first place.

Suppose you're playing $20–$40 hold'em in a fairly aggressive game, and you're holding a real stenchy big blind like J-6 offsuit. Two players limp and the small blind completes, leading you to conclude that nobody has much of anything, for in this game any real hand would have raised. Naturally *you* don't raise; you know what a loser you're holding, and you plan to get away from it as cheaply as possible. Now, though, the flop comes J♠-7♠-6♠, and that changes everything. Now you have an opportunity.

Or do you?

Your analysis tells you that you're not likely to be facing A-big of spades, for that hand, in the hands of these foes, would have come in for a raise. Nor, for the same reason, do you fear J-J. So you start asking yourself what kinds of hands they'd have limped with and still like now, and you get answers like Q-J, J-T suited, 9-8 suited, 7-7, 6-6. Now you're in a pickle. Assuming that you have the best hand (though you may not; someone could be on a set or a weak flush) you really don't want to go around giving away free cards here. But if you *do* bet and they *don't* fold, look at all the potential scare cards you face on the turn. Any spade or straight card will slow you down, and any overcard could give someone a bigger two pair. Further, if you know there's someone downstream capable of making a scare-card bluff, you're really not going to like your spot on the turn. So: Should you bet the flop to protect your hand or check to protect your stack?

Two pair seems like a big holding, but it's a fragile holding, especially since you're out of position, and thus vulnerable to real hands and bluffs/semi-bluffs alike. You might be inclined to bet this hand if you were last to act, but it's unlikely that you'd be last to act holding J-6, for you wouldn't have gotten involved at all if you hadn't been blinded into the pot.

That's the key to this analysis: You were forced in. You posted a blind bet, caught a crap hand, and prepared to kiss your bet goodbye. Thanks to limpers and circumstance, you now seem to be in good shape. But you still only have one bet invested, and you still have a crap hand. A bet from you here is, in essence, an effort to defend your investment, and you have neither the chip commitment nor the card strength to warrant that defense.

Go ahead and check. If someone bets, you can decide whether they have a real hand or you've induced a bluff. Even if you fold winners, it's no heartbreak; good players fold winners every day. Should no one take a stab at the pot on the flop, the turn card may come benign, or even helpful. Now your foes will face a decreased chance of hitting their draws and an increased price for trying, so you can go ahead and bet.

Or, you know, not.

It seems to me that we risk overplaying this hand for a psychological, rather than strategic, reason. When we flop a big hand in the big blind, even a fragile one, we start imagining that we deserve to profit from the hand. For once our blind is not a necessary evil, but rather a choice morsel. That's why we'll protect that fragile holding so aggressively, and in some cases heedlessly. We think we're owed somehow. We're not owed. A blind hand is a blind hand and a crap hand is a crap hand. Maybe we will profit from a strong play here, but we don't *deserve* to profit, any more than we *deserve* to have pocket aces hold up. There is no manifest destiny in poker.

So attend to your underlying motivation here. Are you really trying to maximize your return in this situation, or are you merely trying to cash in on a windfall? If the latter, consider that there may be more to be gained (i.e., not lost) by playing this holding snugly than by playing it aggressively just because you feel you must.

You flop two pair and you bet, right? It's almost automatic.

Except for those times when it's not.

Many excellent hold'em players have their secret stash of favorite moves. Far fewer players have a comprehensive list of vulnerabilities. They may not recognize certain situations as risky, or they may simply be unwilling to admit to their limitations. Don't *you* be unwilling. Spend some time recording your weaknesses and leaknesses. There's real money to be saved in the quest.

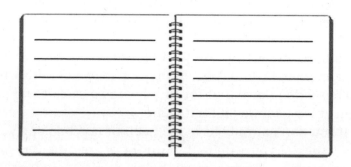

NOTEBOOK

If you're doing your hold'em job right, you're doing more than playing when you play. You're also making observations—detailed discoveries about yourself, your foes, and the play of the game in general. If you're *really* doing your job right, you're writing down these observations: in a Palm, in a notebook, on a napkin. They may not amount to much one by one, but over time, these scrawled notes add up to your overall understanding of the game. If nothing else, every time you record something you've seen, that's an instance of you being awake and alert at the table, and not playing the game by rote. Nor should you be concerned about making discoveries that have been made by others before you, or even by you before. Every time you re-learn something, you cement it that much more firmly in your brain. Here's a note from my notebook:

Learn to win without good cards. It gives you protection against times when you lose with good cards.

This is not a new thought, but thinking it and writing it again there at the table reminded me of the two important instructions it contains. First, seek and exploit targets of opportunity. Second, don't let bad beats get you down. Again, none of this is new, but it's all useful. And there's nothing wrong with being seen by the rest of the table as "that notebook wonk." They may or may not care what you're writing down, but for those who *do* care, it will put them at least a little off their game.

If you don't already have the habit of notebooking your play, I suggest you acquire it. Both the act of discovery and the discoveries themselves will help you play your best.

Here, then, are some recent downloads from my note-book, along with brief commentary.

A Devastating Tell: Turn card completes a four-straight, 8-9-T-J. Lead bettor glances at his cards and bets. Unless he's supremely tricky, how can he not have the straight?

We see this action all the time, and for some strange rea-son, we discount it. We can look at someone looking at his cards, *know for sure* that he has a made hand, and still pay him off. We persuade ourselves that a true tell is a false tell, that he's looking at his cards in an elaborate effort to sell the bluff. But most players don't bluff that way. They don't call attention to themselves. They let their bets do the talk-ing. This player is peeking to confirm to himself that it's okay to bet. Take his action at face value unless and until he gives you reason to believe otherwise. It's less likely that the opponent is supremely tricky than that our own wish-ful thinking is getting in our way.

The Flinch is a tell you can look for. When a scare card hits the board, and a player responds as if struck, his worst fear has been realized.

This is just me reminding myself of something I already know, that scare cards are scary. Someone on a fragile hold-ing, such as the J-6 two pair described earlier, will be keenly aware of the cards that can kill his hand. He's "on the look-out," so to speak, and in this heightened state of awareness, he may just give himself away when a card he hates hits the board. Here we have another strong argument for not watching the cards fall, but rather watching those who watch.

You teach at the table and justify it as misdirection, but you give away more than you gain.

When the first *Killer Poker* book came out, I felt an obsessive need to promote it at the table, and also to back it up with my analysis and wisdom (to justify my author's authority, I suppose). Though I purposely tried to skew that analysis away from the way I really play, I soon realized that I wasn't being nearly as deceptive as I thought I was. Instead, I was revealing key specifics of my strategic and tactical approach to the game. This note reminded me to shut the hell up, and I offer up the same useful advice to you. We like to show off at the table; it's a common enough self-indulgence. But like so many self-indulgences (ice cream, heroin, what-have-you) this one can be costly. Not to put too fine a point on it, if you must talk, lie.

Here's a guy reading The Racing Form at the table? Go after him!

I'm constantly looking for players who are not only not attentive, but actually actively inattentive at the table. Someone who's reading is obviously not giving the game his best. Moreover, someone reading *The Racing Form* informs me that he's a gambler of a certain stripe. As a horse player, he's apt to be a more wide-open poker player than someone who never bets on anything but cards. Here we see the difference between a pure poker player and a gambler who happens to play poker. As my "Go after him!" indicates, I consider the latter to be vulnerable to my assault.

There's a tremendous crossover between poker players and sports bettors. In the main, those cross-bettors are likely to have a little more gamble in them than their poker-exclusive foes. Plan, and play, accordingly.

You can try to be someone who's easy to read, and then train your opponents to read you incorrectly. The trouble is you might, in fact, just be easy to read.

I like the idea of training players. If they're fearful, I try to train them to be more fearful. If they always think I'm bluffing, I'll bend them further that way. This note reminds me, though, that sometimes my efforts backfire on me. I become so demonstrative in my actions and my table talk that I actually give savvy opponents the means to an accurate read. Instead of working so hard to make 'em guess wrong, I should be like Switzerland: remain neutral in word and deed, and let 'em guess wrong on their own.

In low-limit and mid-limit hold'em games, most players can't get away from their hands.

Typical Jim holds A-J. The flop is J-7-7. He bets and gets a call. The turn is an offsuit deuce. He bets and gets raised. He has no reason to believe his opponent is bluff-raising here, and every reason to believe she slowplayed a seven. Yet he calls, gunning for a two-outer, or praying that his foe is driving a worse jack or T-T or 9-9. Typical Jim will call this hand all the way down, because his hope overrules his reason. At showdown, he'll frown at her 8-7 holding and say, "I knew it all along." Don't be a Typical Jim. If you're beat and you know it, fold. Bet with your head, not your hope.

Some guys get animated when they hit their hand. Listen for the sound of "a new county heard from." When a previously silent player starts talking, either he has a hand or the coke kicked in.

Adrenaline is a stimulant. Big cards, with the attendant promise of big pots and big wins, will trigger the release of adrenaline in many players. Under the influence of this drug, people become voluble. Those not schooled in curbing their reaction will give themselves away by their sudden, unexpected yackking. Moral: Don't just watch, listen. When a normally taciturn player starts gabbing, that's the time to get out of the way.

Devaluing the Raise: If you want people to think your raises represent real muscle, you can't raise too promiscuously, or you'll devalue the clout of your own raise. To steal successfully, you have to be able to create the firm feeling that you never bet without the goods.

Here we have a quandary, one with roots in the fact that raises can serve various purposes. Sometimes we raise for the sake of sheer bully behavior. Other times we raise to win the pot right there. One seems to cancel out the other: If they know we're bullies, they may not want to mess with us because we raise so much, but also they'll discount the power of any given raise because, well, because we raise so much. What to do? How about this: Target different opponents for different types of raises. If you're up against someone who can be put off his hand, make your power moves and use his fear to steer him toward folding. If you know someone else has you made as a bluffer, save your raises against that foe for when you have the goods.

The other thing you can think about is "surfing the session." People's opinions of you change over time. If you raise a lot in a short space of hands, you will devalue your raise. This means people will pay you off. When you tighten up, your raises go back up in value, meaning you can steal. Ride your session like riding a wave. Always ask yourself, *What value does my raise have now?* From that vantage point, you can bet according to your foes' perception of your power and/or start to adjust their perception by speeding up or slowing down.

The way you pick up your cards can be a tell before you even look at them.

If someone's been running bad, or hasn't been holding cards, he starts to get frustrated and fatalistic, and these emotions are then revealed in the way he picks up his hand. In his normal state of mind, he cups and peeks, careful not to let other players see what he has. As his mood plummets, he becomes more careless. He lifts his cards higher and looks at them savagely, almost defiantly, as if to say, "What's the point of protecting this hand when it's just going to be another crap hand anyway?" The way he handles his hand tells you much about his state of mind, and even the value of his hand. Suppose he gives his cards a "bad mood" look, but then sets them down carefully and covers them with chips. He has no intention of folding. He has picked up a hand at last.

Or possibly only half a hand. Remember, most players' starting requirements go down if they've been getting jack-three to death. In his feral state, this player may be determined to make Q-T play like A-A. I think there's more to be gained by getting out of his way than by going to war here, even if you know his hand has only middling value. First of all, you don't want him getting well at your expense. Second, if he gets no action, his *I can't catch cards* negativity will be reinforced by *and when I do I don't get paid.* Keep this foe glowering. He's easier to control and easier to beat. Rather than match his loose call with a loose call of your own here, wait for a big hand and let his loose call walk into your raise. This player is on the hook. You don't have to land him all at once.

Go to School on That: When you see a player call along with J-J into a board showing A-Q-x-x-x, GTSOT. He's telling you that he'll call with scant hope and therefore is bluff-proof.

It's most likely a mistake for J-J to call a flop of A-Q-x, and it's quite ridiculous to call along to the river if there's any kind of action. If you wanted to bluff this foe, you'd need to be able to count on him to come to his senses and sensibly fold. Mostly, though, you can't count on players playing correctly. Mostly you don't want to count on that because if they're generally playing correctly, you're probably in the wrong game. Try to be the only one playing correctly in a generally incorrect game, but recognize that playing correctly means seeing things as they are. If a player has demonstrated his willingness to cling to big underpairs and you haven't gone to school on that, you have no one to blame but yourself when your attempt to bluff him fails.

Don't put yourself in a situation where you have to hit the flop twice to continue.

You're in late position. There's a bet and a raise in front of you, and you're trying to decide whether to jump in. It's a good idea to pause and ponder what kind of flop you're looking for. If you call along with something like K-8, you won't be able to drive the hand (nor probably even safely continue) unless you hit twice: K-K-x, 8-8-x, or K-8-x. Those double-hit flops are rare—but not so rare in our minds. Filtering expectation through hope, we anticipate hitting the flop we need. Next time you're faced with a call you know you probably shouldn't make, just ask yourself if you need to hit twice to drive. If the answer is yes, toss the hand away.

Are you having a luxury crisis, JV? How real is the problem you're having now?

Once I worked for a television network in Sydney, Australia. Every Wednesday, the network flew me down to Melbourne to oversee a situation comedy that was taping there. It was a short flight, just one hour, but first class both ways. One night I got to the Melbourne airport late. I didn't miss the flight back to Sydney, but I did get bumped back from first class to the main cabin. I hit the roof! How dared they treat me this way?! Didn't they know who I was?! I was a *businessman,* for Pete's sake, and a Network Suit at that! When I got back to Sydney and grumbled to my wife that I had to sit in *coach* the whole way home, her sardonic smile introduced me to the concept of the *luxury crisis.*

I can have a luxury crisis any time I forget that I don't really have it so bad. Some waiter takes away my table-side tray of food before I'm done—luxury crisis! Or I come running back from the bathroom, yelling, "I'm in, I'm in!" but the dealer mucks my hand (undoubtedly pocket aces)—luxury crisis! Once I ranted for ten minutes because someone stole my crossword puzzle. Why was I doing a crossword puzzle at the poker table anyway? Needless to say, the dark outlook of a luxury crisis can throw me off my game.

Could it happen to you, too? If so, keep the concept of luxury crisis alive in your mind to remind yourself of your real position in this world. Whether you play poker professionally or recreationally, it is, in a sense, a privilege you owe to circumstance. You have the time and money to spend doing this; you're not off working in some salt mine or smelter. Use this awareness the next time a luxury crisis sneaks up on you.

Heavens! There's no cream in my coffee! Porter!

Can it really be this simple? "Know your foes better than they know you and you can't possibly lose."

Can it really be that simple? I'm starting to think it can. Hold'em is a game of incomplete information, but information doesn't exist simply in a yes/no state. Rather, we have a *continuum of information,* a set of suppositions and firm facts about every opponent we face. Likewise, our foes have suppositions and facts about us. If we do a better job of manipulating their knowledge than they do of manipulating ours, we must, in the long run, make money on the margin. This is an extension of the idea of forcing inferior decision-makers to make lots of decisions. If you can get your opponents to make correct decisions *based on incorrect information,* you'll achieve the same result. This is why it's so important to monitor not just how you read your opponents but also how they currently read you.

Afterword

You don't need to be what you need to be, JV.
You just need to be what you are.

I wrote these words after a disastrous night playing poker
and found them recently in an old notebook. I present
them here because I think they may mean as much to you
in your circumstance as they meant to me in mine. First, let
me set the scene.

I had been invited to lecture on a poker cruise. Well, let
me tell you that really floated my boat, for it combined so
many of my favorite things: public speaking, free travel,
exotic destinations, and lots and lots and lots of poker.
Aboard ship, I found that everyone knew who I was, and
everyone was eager to hear what I had to say about poker. I
had come a long way from that scandalously under-attended
presentation at the Maxim in Las Vegas so many years before. I felt confident that I could deliver the goods. I was
prepared to give this audience what they wanted: useful information presented in an entertaining fashion. And I did.
I knocked 'em dead. People bought my books; they asked
for autographs. I felt like a star.

That's the problem. I felt like a star.

Because then I went to play poker.

And I wasn't myself. I was that star. I stopped being a poker player and morphed into a strange new creature, a *poker luminary*. You don't have to tell me that my priorities were all screwed up. I know that now, and I even knew it then, but there are other buzzes than the poker buzz, you know, and it was the celebrity buzz that strung me out that day. Instead of playing good, solid Killer Poker, I was determined to play stylish, elegant, look-at-me-world Killer Poker! Can you imagine all the death-defying mistakes I made? Would you like to see the list? I happen to have it here, for I recorded it in my notebook during the subsequent long, dark (and slightly seasick) nighttime of my soul.

No, seriously, John, what were you thinking? You raised with weak aces. You raised with lots worse than weak aces. You defended every blind. You raised with bottom pair again and again and again. You took inside straight draws. You check-raise bluffed into obvious strength. You did everything in your power to call attention to yourself—everything, that is, except play well. I ask again: Dude, what were you thinking?

Practitioners of improvisational comedy note a phenomenon called "shining." When an improv actor is shining, he's not concerned with creating a successful scene or with making the experience rewarding to the audience or his fellow actors. He's only interested in shining so brightly on stage that no one can tear their eyes away. I'm sure you see this for what it is: an act of pure ego.

That's what I was doing that day on that cruise. I was shining. Well, trying to. Actually, I was having my ass handed to me in a bilge bucket. You might argue that this was inevitable since everyone was gunning for me, inspired to go big against a motivational speaker who had recently charged them with that very mission: *Go big or go home.* To which I reply, *yeah, maybe.* Sure, some people played well against me because they cranked up their concentration, but others in equal numbers played poorly against me because they were cowed (completely wrongly as it turns out) by my minor celebrity status.

No, they didn't beat me. *I* beat me. And I did a damn good job.

I don't dwell on that experience these days. I know about review and regret. I know about the muddy road. I know how to let go. But I raise the subject here because it points out the fundamental truth that, hey, we all have our faults. We lead ourselves into traps all the time, traps that we fail to recognize or, having recognized them, nevertheless choose to ignore.

No matter how bad a game is, you can leave it. Unless you convince yourself you can beat it.

No matter how bad a hand is, you can fold it. Unless you persuade yourself that your skills make it playable.

No matter how tilty you've been, you can straighten up. Unless you deny you're on tilt or simply cease to care.

No matter how many holes your game has, you can fill them. Unless pride makes them vanish from your sight.

You don't need to be what you need to be. You don't need to be a world champion today. You don't need to play at stratospheric limits. You don't need to quit your day job. You only need to be what you are. A poker practitioner. A student of the craft. Someone determined to make the most of this session, this hand, and this bet. You don't need to impress anyone: not your loved ones, not other players, not even yourself. You just need to do your best.

Hold'em is a tricky business. The choice between folding or raising preflop may rest on nothing larger than the twitch of a wrist of a player downstream. The choice between calling or folding on the river may stand on a pile of factors including the size of the pot, size of the field, players' images, players' history, and more—and you still might not get it right. If anyone tells you they know what to do 100 percent of the time in any hold'em situation, they're either lying or not thinking clearly. The more we study hold'em, the more we realize that what they say is true: It's a game that takes ten minutes to learn and a lifetime to master.

But what a great way to spend ten minutes or a lifetime, huh?

When I started writing this book, I was aware that the subject of how to play hold'em has not gone exactly unexamined in recent years. Poker exploration has become, in a sense, like ocean exploration. There are no new oceans to be discovered in this world of ours; if you want to learn new things, you have to go deeper. In this book I've tried to go deeper—deeper into my own analysis and understanding, and deeper into strategies for thinking more effectively about the game.

But there's one thing I've discovered about going deeper: *It's murky down there!* When deconstructing hold'em and hold'em situations, it's pitifully easy to find occasions when two (or three!) opposite and conflicting strategies each (or all!) make perfect sense. If you're holding A-9 on the button, for example, and it's folded around to you, you could make a case for folding *or* calling *or* raising. It depends on how you want to play the hand.

No. It depends on your goals for the game. If you want a snug, little, low-risk session, you might not get involved with that A-9. If you want to run the table, you're going to push in there with a raise. At the end of the day, I don't know you. I don't know your style of play and I don't know the foes you face. Which is not to disclaim the strategies and tactics I've outlined in this book; they work for me and I stand by them. At the same time, I think that strategy and tactics are fundamentally less important than overall approach to the game. The individual tools, to put it another way, don't matter so much as the craftsman's commitment to toolcraft. Think deeply and clearly about your hold'em. Whatever conclusions you reach will probably be right, merely as a function of all that deep, clear thought.

Which brings me to a story.

There was a small Jewish community in Poland before the Second World War. A famous rabbi taught there, and the fundamental lesson he taught was "Life is like the ocean." Year after year his eager rabbinical students absorbed and repeated this wisdom. "Life is like the ocean," they would say. "Life is like the ocean."

One young student named Daniel was profoundly moved by this truth. It sustained him through the dark years of the Holocaust, actually fueling the faith that helped him survive. After the war, he moved to America and became a well-respected rabbi in his own right. "Life is like the ocean," he would tell his students, and "Life is like the ocean," they would agree.

However, one day a young scholar came up to him and asked, "Rabbi, why is life like the ocean?" Daniel found that he had no answer, and this shook him to the core of his being. He had believed so deeply for so many years that life was like the ocean and now, suddenly, the words had lost all meaning. He did his best to quell his distress, but it ate at him like a cancer.

*So he took a trip. He returned to his home village in Po-
land. He had no reason to believe that his old teacher was
still alive and living there, but nevertheless he felt com-
pelled to go back and ask, if he could, "Why is life like the
ocean?"*

*Well, against all foreseeable odds, the old rabbi had sur-
vived the Holocaust and had returned to his village. Finding him there on his deathbed, Daniel leaned in close and
whispered with a fierce urgency, "Rabbi, Rabbi, I must know:
Why is life like the ocean?"*

*The old man looked up at him with rheumy eyes. For a
long time he didn't speak. "Okay," he said at last, "so life
isn't like the ocean."*

In hold'em, as in life, there's often more than one right
answer. Our job in all cases, it seems to me, is somehow to
find our own.

I hope you've enjoyed reading this book. I've certainly
enjoyed writing it. I've learned a thing or two about myself
and my hold'em along the way, and I trust that you have,
too. The one thing I know more than anything is you have
to stay present in the game. There are certainly times when
you can run programs or scripts with a reasonable expectation of success, but there's no substitute for just actively
thinking about the game while the game is going on. Stay
flexible. Stay loose. Stay alive in your mind. Remember that
hold'em is a game of decisions; decisions based on information that comes at you in a steady stream. Remember
that the first answer to any question is "It depends," and
that there are no hard and fast rules about anything.

Except pocket aces. Definitely raise with those.

Glossary

Bevvies. Beverages. Alcoholic drinks.

Blind weevil. Someone who attacks way more than his share of blinds.

Bluff-outs. Scare cards; cards that hit highly coordinated flops, such as a fourth suited card, and can be used to represent drawing hands that got there.

Clang-clang. Runner-runner bricks; a combination of turn and river cards that fail to improve fruitful flush or straight draws.

Clueless parade. A game where people either don't know or don't care about proper poker play. The worst player in this game is known as *the last float in the clueless parade.*

Doubledraw. A card that yields both a flush draw and an open-ended straight draw, such as a turn card Q♠ when you're holding A♠-T♠ and the flop was J♣-9♥-3-♠.

Drunk devaluator. A sliding scale on which the amount a person has had to drink is inversely proportional to the real strength of his hand.

Dry draw. A straight or flush draw that misses.

241

Fakiac. A selectively aggressive player who uses a maniac's image to disguise the true quality of his play.

Fock. Alternative spelling for a penalty word.

Fold-out. A circumstance where all callers surrender to the original preflop raiser on the flop or the turn.

Fossil. An old, old rock.

Game frame. A player's state of mind. When you're in good game frame, you have focus, alertness, and awareness working for you. When you're in bad game frame, you should probably play Pac-Man.

Gift card. When no one bets and everyone sees the next card for free, that's a gift card.

Gravel. Bad cards.

GTSOT. Go to School on That. Observe your foes' patterns of behavior. How they've acted in the past tells you how they'll act in the future, but only if you stay in school.

Junk raise. A raise with bad cards, aimed at wheelhouse players and intended to provide control of any non-high-card flop.

Leakness. Holes in a player's play.

Lemmy. Lemming; a tight, timid, straightforward player who can be easily led to his own demise.

Orphan pot. When everyone checks, the pot is officially an orphan. Adopt it if you can.

Muscle bluff. Also known as a semi-bluff. You don't have the best hand, but you do have something. Contrast with *naked bluff*, a bluff with nothing.

Neeny. A weak, passive play; a needy weenie, if you will.

Nose is open. So stuck in a game that you no longer care how stuck you are, nor how much more you lose. Derived from boxing, where a fighter with his nose open is bleeding and on the way down.

Predictive tell. A tell that lets you anticipate how a foe will react to a certain card-fall.

Pumpkin. An all-around bad player.

Punishment raise. A raise designed to punish promiscuous callers, especially those who'll throw good money after bad.

Quit winners. Come out ahead for a session. Savvy players always tell others they quit winners because they know that short-term outcomes are irrelevant, but a winner's image is worth gold, or anyway, bets.

Rebuy fever. A tournament affliction wherein a player ends up making rebuy after rebuy, far out of proportion to the size of the tournament payout.

ROI. Return on Investment; shorthand for the relationship between card odds and pot odds. If you're on a 3 to 1 draw and the pot is offering a 5 to 1 payout, you have fat ROI.

Show-and-tell. The ego-driven compulsion that some players have to show their cards when they make a big laydown. Mostly they're just showing their flaws.

Stealth ace. A perceptual phenomenon where an ace on the flop becomes virtually invisible to the player holding K-K.

String cheese. Loosely connected bad cards.

Sub-basement. A pocket pair lower than all the cards on board.

True value. An image that suggests you generally have the hand you represents. Selling this image persuasively can lead to bluffing opportunities.

Unbuttoned. Way too loose. A player who calls all the time is said to be completely unbuttoned.

Wheelhouse. The hold'em playing zone: cards between ten and ace. Many lemmy players will call with any two wheelhouse cards.

Notes

Here's a place to record your own hold'em thoughts, questions, observations, or discoveries. Go nuts! I'll start you off with this little poser:

The problem is not: playing hold'em;
The problem is: not playing hold'em.

_____

_____

_____

_____

_____

_____

_____

_____

About the Author

John Vorhaus has written more than a million words about poker, a fact he finds quite astounding. When not writing about poker or playing poker, he writes screenplays and television shows, and travels the world teaching others how to do likewise. His seminal book on comedy writing, *The Comic Toolbox,* has inspired thousands of writers and will be drawing down royalties for somebody long after John is dead. Someone once asked him if he was an inveterate poker player. "Not inveterate," he replied. "More like *veterate.*" He's still not sure what that means.

He lives in Monrovia, California, with his wife, Maxx Duffy, and his dogs, Dodger and Ranger. He lives online at www.vorza.com, and welcomes your comments at jv@vorza.com.